SOMETHING TO TIDE YOU OVER

In *The Stand*, what was the name of the twenty-two-year-old deaf-mute who was born in Caslin, Nebraska?

True or false: "The Plant" is an abandoned Stephen King novel-in-progress.

In the short story "Battleground," from the *Night Shift* collection, who saw the nuclear flash when the soldiers nuked Renshaw?

In *The Gunslinger*, how did the man in black appear to the gunslinger in the mountains?

When was Stephen King born, and which of his fictional characters shares the same birthday?

THE STEPHEN KING
QUIZ BOOK

STEPHEN SPIGNESI is the author of *The Shape Under the Sheet: The Complete Stephen King Encyclopedia* and *Mayberry, My Hometown,* a highly regarded look at the *Andy Griffith Show*. He is married and lives in New Haven, Connecticut.

D0830536

UNCOVER THE KEY TO THE MIND AND
METHOD OF THE MASTER OF MACABRE

STEPHEN KING:
THE ART OF DARKNESS

by
Douglas E. Winter

Stephen King. Scaring us to death has made him the most popular writer of all time, with over 82 million copies of his books in print worldwide. Now, in this first authoritative book on King's life and fiction, we get a thought-provoking look at the master storyteller who turned horror into a national pastime. With behind-the-scenes details of how each work was conceived and written, including an in-depth analysis of *The Stand, The Dark Tower: The Gunslinger, 'Salem's Lot, Firestarter, The Shining,* and many others, and an exclusive interview with King on *Pet Sematary,* this fascinating book brings the "Master of the Macabre" vividly to life.

"Outstanding . . . a rewarding study of King and his work that can be read for its own literary quality."
—*Washington Post Book World*

"Winter has taught me things about the novels of Stephen King, just when I was sure that was no longer possible."
—Peter Straub

"King fans most definitely will want to add this comprehensive book to their collection."   —*UPI*

Buy it at your local bookstore or use this convenient coupon for ordering.

NEW AMERICAN LIBRARY
P.O. Box 999, Bergenfield, New Jersey 07621

Please send me _____ copies of *Stephen King: The Art of Darkness* (0-451-16674-0) $4.50 plus $1.00 postage and handling per order. I enclose ☐ check ☐ money order (no C.O.D.'s or cash), or charge my ☐ Mastercard ☐ VISA.

Card # _____ Exp. Date _____

Signature _____

Name_____

Address_____

City _____ State _____ Zip Code _____

Allow a minimum of 4-6 weeks for delivery.
This offer, prices and numbers are subject to change without notice.

THE
STEPHEN KING
Q·U·I·Z
B·O·O·K

STEPHEN SPIGNESI

A SIGNET BOOK

SIGNET
Published by the Penguin Group
Penguin Books USA Inc., 375 Hudson Street,
New York, New York 10014, U.S.A.
Penguin Books Ltd, 27 Wrights Lane,
London W8 5TZ, England
Penguin Books Australia Ltd, Ringwood,
Victoria, Australia
Penguin Books Canada Ltd, 2801 John Street,
Markham, Ontario, Canada L3R 1B4
Penguin Books (N.Z.) Ltd, 182-190 Wairau Road,
Auckland 10, New Zealand

Penguin Books Ltd, Registered Offices:
Harmondsworth, Middlesex, England

First published by Signet, an imprint of Penguin Books USA Inc.
division of Penguin Books USA Inc.

First Printing, August, 1990
10 9 8 7 6 5 4 3 2 1

Copyright © Stephen Spignesi, 1990
All rights reserved

REGISTERED TRADEMARK—MARCA REGISTRADA

Printed in the United States of America

Without limiting the rights under copyright reserved above, no part of this
publication may be reproduced, stored in or introduced into a retrieval
system, or transmitted, in any form, or by any means (electronic, mechanical,
photocopying, recording, or otherwise), without the prior written permission
of both the copyright owner and the above publisher of this book.

BOOKS ARE AVAILABLE AT QUANTITY DISCOUNTS WHEN USED TO PROMOTE PRODUCTS
OR SERVICES. FOR INFORMATION PLEASE WRITE TO PREMIUM MARKETING DIVISION,
PENGUIN BOOKS USA INC., 375 HUDSON STREET, NEW YORK, NEW YORK 10014.

For Pam

CONTENTS

Introduction

I went to a Catholic grammar school where I was taught by a bunch of repressed nuns, and then went on to a Catholic high school where I was taught by a bunch of repressed brothers, but if I put aside my teachers' psychosexual hangups, one thing I'll admit about my early education is that it was top drawer.

Our curriculum was always at least two years ahead of the local public schools, and even though I now look back at those years and remember the Extra-Strength Catholic guilt and repression, the education I got in that twelve-year period has served me well ever since.

One incident has always stood out in my mind, and as I was preparing to write this Introduction, the memory of this long-dead drama flashed through my consciousness, vivid and real, in a millisecond.

It was the first day of my sophomore year.

My classmates and I were working our way through our new schedules, finding rooms, meeting teachers, and deciding which faculty members would be on the receiving end of merciless torture for the entire semester, and which teachers were all right. (One English teacher named Howie immediately ingratiated himself to us by entering the room, slamming his briefcase down on the desk, reaching into it and pulling out a comic book. "The big news of the day is that the new *Fantastic Four* is on the stands," he announced. "It's a good one." We were floored. This was the same guy who pronounced "fog" with a soft G (it came out "foj") and who assigned us Bernard Malumud's *The Natural* and almost got fired for it because the book contained a very tame description of a woman's nipple. Remember what I said about repressed? If you're out there, Howie, thanks a lot. You did a lot of good, and I learned a lot from you.)

In any case, Biology 101 was on my class schedule that day, and the class took place on the first floor of the building.

The teacher was a short, dark, and intense brother named Brother Theodore who looked like a heavyset Woody Allen with a pompadour. He even had the black horn-rimmed glasses. (And no, he wasn't the bizarre stand-up comic who wears Ban-Lon shirts and appears on David Letterman, although the comic Brother Theodore would have certainly felt at home at my high school.)

Brother Theodore walked in the room, told us to shut up, and read us the riot act. (Brothers didn't play. They would just as soon kick the shit out of you as look at you.)

Then he made an announcement that has stayed with me all these years, and that came to my mind when thinking about this introduction.

"I am now going to tell you what will be on your final exam."

Our ears perked up. Was he kidding, or what? It was the *first day* of class!

"Your final exam will be an open book exam," he continued. (We liked the sound of "open book." It sounded somehow like sanctioned cheating. It had to be easier than committing everything to memory, right?) "Your exam will consist of one question, and one question only. This question consists of two words and can be answered in twenty-five words or less, and you can bring not only your textbooks to the final, but any and all other reference books you so desire."

This was getting better by the minute.

"The final will comprise 50 percent of your grade."

We winced. We started to realize that this guy was serious. After all, 50 percent of *anything* was a lot, and if the question could be answered in twenty-five words or less, then it had to be a lot tougher than we would have liked.

"If any of you can correctly answer this question now, you may leave my class, not attend another session for the rest of the semester, and I will record an A as your grade for the course."

That sounded good. Our pencils hovered over the notebooks, and I'm sure fantasies of a free period every day for the next four months flitted through every adolescent brain cell in that room.

"The final exam question is this: 'Define life.' "

We stared at the Woodman.

He continued. "And allow me to give you this caution: The fact that this is a Catholic institution does not mean squat in my classroom. If a deity of any sort is mentioned or referred to in any way, shape, or form in your answer, you will immediately fail this course and I will see you in summer school. And this building is not air-conditioned, gentlemen."

I ended up with a B for the course.

I got a C on the final because I missed three or four points of the answer.

It turned out Brother Theodore was looking for a very specific answer detailing the biological definition of life—as covered in his class. Any old dictionary definition would not do. DNA was in there, as was reproduction, and the evolutionary mechanism.

I probably don't remember 10 percent of what I learned in his class—but I remembered that question, and I also remembered suddenly understanding that "open book" does not mean "a piece of cake."

I tell that story as part of the introduction to *The Stephen King Quiz Book* to make the point that rote memorization is not learning.

It is nothing.

I spent the semester *thinking* about that question.

For the first time in my life, I realized that solving a problem through thought and logic, discernment and rational thinking did more teaching than ten years of flawlessly accurate memorization could ever do.

The Stephen King Quiz Book contains 107 quizzes totaling 1,510 questions—and they are all "open book" quizzes.

My hope is that they will lead you back to the Stephen King work from which the questions are drawn, and stimulate you to read deeper, thereby enhancing your enjoyment of the Titan of Terror's work.

Don't just take the quizzes to see how many correct answers you can get.

Instead, answer the questions you can, and then go back and reread the work, looking for the answers you missed.

My sophomore year of high school was one of the most intellectually stimulating periods of my life. Why? Because I was on a quest to not only answer the final exam question correctly, but to understand *why* Brother Theodore's twenty-five words or less were the *right* twenty-five words or less.

The quizzes in *The Stephen King Quiz Book* were designed to be fun, challenging, and just one more way of enjoying the work of our favorite writer of all time, Stephen Edwin King. (And no, "What is Stephen King's middle name?" is not one of the questions!)

I sincerely tried to make the questions entertaining, while still being as specific as possible with the material covered. There were many cases where I either rewrote or scrapped a question that I thought was too vague and that didn't have a definite, "it could only be this" answer.

The Stephen King Quiz Book is in ten sections:

• Parts I and II cover King's life and the front matter of his books.

• Part III covers King's novels. There are quizzes for all of King's novels, beginning with *Carrie* and continuing up through *The Dark Half*, his most recent release.

• Part IV includes quizzes on the *Night Shift* stories,

the *Different Seasons* novellas, and the *Skeleton Crew* stories.

• Part V consists of quizzes on selected uncollected Stephen King short stories. I've included quizzes only for stories that I felt were relatively easy to locate, and I have listed what I felt were the most accessible sources for these tales in the Bibliography. This section bears very little resemblance to the original section I had proposed to New American Library. That early draft of this section included quizzes on extremely rare King stories— stories that are extremely difficult to locate, and in cases of the early stories, downright impossible.

I had written quizzes for "People, Places, and Things," "The Star Invaders," "I Was a Teenage Grave Robber," "The Glass Floor," "Slade," and even *The Plant.* I wrote *The Stephen King Quiz Book* while writing my other book about King, *The Shape Under the Sheet: The Complete Stephen King Encyclopedia*, and I think that my total immersion in even the rarest of King's work figuratively put blinders on me. Because I knew about all this stuff, I figured *everybody*—even the most casual of King's fans—knew what I knew.

A conversation with my editor, Matt Sartwell, opened my eyes, so to speak, and made me realize that the majority of King's fans are mostly familiar with his mainstream work: the novels, the story collections and, yes, the movies. After all, we reasoned, these "hidden horrors" were one of the reasons I was writing *The Shape Under the Sheet*, wasn't it? So I hope that Part V isn't too frustrating for those of you who don't have these tales. Either hunt them down via the Bibliography and the listing of sources in the back of this book, or cheat, learn the answers, and then impress your friends with your knowledge of King "obscura!"

• Part VI covers the five Bachman novels, beginning with *Rage* and ending with *Thinner.*

• Part VII covers the two published volumes of King's *Dark Tower* epic, *The Gunslinger* and *The Drawing of the Three*, both of which are now widely available in inexpensive NAL editions.

• Part VIII quizzes you on the *Creepshow* stories, and includes some details on the original text versions of

"The Lonesome Death of Jordy Verrill" ("Weeds"), and "The Crate" ("The Crate").

• Part IX consists of quizzes on the later short stories—those uncollected stories that have appeared in either recent anthologies or, in the case of "Rainy Season," a magazine (*Midnight Graffiti*—see the Bibliography). These uncollected stories should be very easy to find, because the anthologies are still in print, and many are available in libraries. But again, I had to make some choices as to what to leave in and what to leave out.

My original outline had included the relatively unknown short story "The End of the Whole Mess," a story that originally appeared in the October 1986 issue of *Omni* magazine. The story would have been more widely read but for the fact that *Omni* did not include Stephen King's name on the cover of the issue. It was an anniversary issue, and so I guess there wasn't room for another slug. The magazine is still available from the sources listed in the back of this book, and I recommend you buy it first to read, and second to fill out your King collection. It's a somewhat bizarre, experimental tale about "good intentions gone awry," and as the main character deteriorates, his language becomes more primitive—akin to the mental decay of Charlie in the short story "Flowers for Algernon." The last paragraph of the story reads:

"I have a Bobby his nayme is bruther and I theen I am dun riding and I have a bocks to put this into thats Bobby sd full of quiyet air to last a milyun yrz so gudbo Im goin to stob gadbo bobby i love you it wuz nt yor falt i love you forgiv yu
love you
sined (for the wurld),
Bow Wow Fornoy"

"The End of the Whole Mess" is one of King's somewhat infrequent forays into science fiction, and is worth reading and owning. Check it out.

I have included recent stories in Part IX, all of which are readily available. The most difficult to find will probably be "My Pretty Pony," since there were only 15,000 copies of the trade edition published. But I know it's available from both the Overlook Connection and Michael J. Autrey, and I'm sure that some of those 15,000 copies ended up in libraries across the country. Use the interlibrary loan service and you should be able to find a copy.

The last section of quizzes, Part X, consists of miscellaneous quizzes covering all kinds of gruesome thingies. Part X will ask you to "Match the Monsters" and to also come up with the way certain King characters met their demise. There are matching quizzes, true or false questions, and multiple-choice quizzes. There is a particularly difficult "brand name" fill-in-the-blanks quiz, and a final "Show No Mercy and Take No Prisoners" quiz.

The book concludes with a Bibliography and a directory of sources.

I think it says a lot about the work of Stephen King that we as readers would care so much about his tales that we'd want to take quizzes testing our knowledge of the minutae of the Stephen Kingdom.

The work of Stephen King is important to us: It takes us away, it entertains, it educates, but most important—!!!IT SCARES US!!!

Okay.

Here comes the part most of you can (and will!) skip over: The Dreaded Acknowledgments Section!

My deepest thanks and appreciation must go out to the following:

• My wife, Pam, for her continued belief in me and my ridiculous and boundless dreams;

• My mother, the amazing Lee, for her unbelievable help above and beyond, and for being my mother;

• Dave Hinchberger, for being such a friend that he was the first person I had to call when I got the contract for this book;

• My Popular Culture, Ink. editor Tom Schultheiss, for his advice, support, and encouragement, both for *The Stephen King Quiz Book* and *The Shape Under the Sheet*;

• My agent, John White, for helping in ways too numerous to mention and/or count, and for his friendship;

• My editor, Matt Sartwell, for his help, advice, and friendship;

• Elaine Koster, for her belief in the seductiveness of quizzes;

• My friend, George Beahm, for all his help and support;

• Jerry Williamson and Stan Wiater, for their continual encouragement, friendship, and always (and in all ways) kind words;

• Stephanie and Jim Leonard, Shirley Sonderegger, Doug Winter, Chris Spruce, and Jessie Horsting, for all their help;

• Paul, Laura, David, Maureen, and all their glorious progeny, Jennifer, Amanda, and Joey, for the "mini-vacations" I enjoy when I'm with them all;

• Frank Mandato, Janet and Jerry, Pete, Toni, and the whole crew at Dante's Inferno, Ken Owens, Mark and Paula Savo, Gary Dermer, Katherine Flickinger, Dolores, Tony, Linda, and Sheryl Fantarella, Jay Halpern, Rick Hautala (read this guy, he's terrific!), Steve and Marge Rapuano, and John "Dude" Polisky, all for either help, encouragement, and/or interest;

and especially—(Anton, a drum roll please?)

• The Master Himself, Stephen King, for his continued support for both *The Stephen King Quiz Book* and *The Shape Under the Sheet*, and for his lifelong body of work, without which . . .

That's it.
Now sharpen your pencil, turn the page, and let the quizzes begin!!

STEPHEN
SPIGNESI
May 1990
New Haven, Connecticut

I

THE LIFE AND TIMES OF
STEPHEN KING

THE LIFE AND TIMES OF STEPHEN KING

Quiz 1
A Biographical Quiz

Stephen King has had an amazing life. His talents, imagination, and diligence surfaced at a very early age, and his publishing record is an American legend.

This quiz is a potpourri of questions about King's life, publishing history, education, and fandom. (Many of the answers can be found in Doug Winter's terrific biography/appreciation *Stephen King: The Art of Darkness*. Other valuable sources for biographical information include King's own *Danse Macabre*, the many published interviews with King—*Bare Bones* being the most notable collection of such interviews—the afterwords to his books, and the countless magazine articles about his career. (See the Bibliography.)

1. Where was Stephen King born?
2. When was Stephen King born, and which of his fictional characters shares the same birthday?
3. What were the names of Stephen King's parents?
4. What is the name of Stephen King's wife?
5. Where do Stephen King and his family live?
6. Who was Stephen King's coauthor for the 1960 collection "People, Places, and Things"?
7. Who was Richard Bachman?
8. What was the name of the official Stephen King newsletter?
9. What was the title of the first short story King ever had published?
10. What was the title of the first short story King ever sold?
11. Where did Stephen King go to college?
12. What are the names of Stephen King's children?

13. What was the title and year of release of the first novel King ever published?
14. Stephen King has appeared in five films. Name them.
15. What is Stephen King's favorite baseball team?
16. Who were the three primary influences on Stephen King's writing?
17. What is the name of the publishing company that published King's *Dark Tower* books in their limited editions?
18. What is the name of Stephen King's own publishing company?
19. What national news magazine featured King on the cover in 1986?
20. What are the two publishing companies that will be publishing King's books in hardcover and softcover through 1993?

II

"PAGE ONE"

Quiz 2

Stephen King loves to start off his work with quotes from other writers. These epigraphs often add layers of meaning to the work you're about to read (or reread in most cases). Your mission (if you choose to accept it) is to identify the Stephen King work that contains the following epigraphs, and if you can, the original author of the quote. (Without looking it up in the King work in which it appeared, that is!). Good luck!

1. "Tout s'en va, tout passe, l'eau coule, et le coeur oublie."
2. "I would encourage every American to walk as often as possible. It's more than healthy; it's fun."
3. "The sleep of reason breeds monsters."
4. "O Lord, won't you buy me a Mercedes-Benz? My friends all drive Porsches, I must make amends . . ."
5. "I slept and I dreamed the dream. This time there was no disguise anywhere. I was the malicious male-female dwarf figure, the principle of joy-in-destruction; and Saul was my counterpart, male-female, my brother and my sister, and we were dancing in some open place, under enormous white buildings, which were filled with hideous, menacing, black machinery which held destruction. But in the dream, he and I, or she and I, were friendly, we were not hostile, we were together in spiteful malice. There was a terrible yearning nostalgia in the dream, the longing for death. We came together and kissed, in love. It was terrible, and even in the dream I knew it. Because I recognised in the dream those

7

other dreams we all have, when the essence of love, of tenderness, is concentrated into a kiss or a caress, but now it was the caress of two half-human creatures, celebrating destruction."

6. "About suffering they were never wrong,
The Old Masters: how well they understood
Its human position; how it takes place
While someone else is eating or opening a window or just walking dully along . . ."

7. "Writing does not *cause* misery, it is born of misery."

8. "Jesus said to them, 'Our friend Lazarus sleeps, but I go, that I may awake him out of his sleep.' Then the disciples looked at each other, and some smiled because they did not know Jesus had spoken in a figure. 'Lord, if he sleeps, he shall do well.' So then Jesus spoke to them more plainly, 'Lazarus is dead, yes . . . nevertheless let us go to him.' "

9. "Tell you now that the whole town is empty."

10. "I heard it through the grapevine."

11. "Out of the blue and into the black."

12. "Learn to work the saxophone,
I play just what I feel,
Drink Scotch whiskey
All night long,
And die behind the wheel."

13. "Outside the street's on fire
In a real death waltz
Between what's flesh and what's fantasy
And the poets down here
Don't write nothing at all
They just stand back and let it all be
And in the quick of the night
They reach for their moment
And try to make an honest stand . . ."

14. "Meet revenge is proper and just."

15. "Thirty days hath September,
April, June, and November,
all the rest but the Second have thirty-one,
Rain and snow and jolly sun,
and the moon grows fat in every one."

16. "Well, when Tom and me got to the edge of the hilltop, we looked away down into the village and could see three or four lights twinkling, where there was sick folks, may be; and stars over us was sparkling ever so fine; and down by the village was the river, a whole mile broad, and awful still and grand."

17. "What was the worst thing you've ever done?"

   "I won't tell you that, but I'll tell you the worst thing that ever happened to me . . . the most dreadful thing . . ."

18. "You don't fuck around with the infinite."

19. "Then he ran all the way to town, screamin 'It came out of the sky!' "

20. "You will have thirty seconds, and please remember that your answer must be in the form of a question."

OPENERS

Quiz 3

This quiz tests your knowledge of Stephen King's "Openers"—the first lines of his novels, short stories, and poetry. For each opener, identify the work it begins.

1. "Do you love?"
2. "Jack Torrance thought: *Officious little prick.*"
3. "She was squinting at the thermometer in the white light coming through the window."
4. "Miss Sidley was her name, and teaching was her game."
5. "They had been predicting a norther all week long and along about Thursday we got it, a real screamer that piled up eight inches by four in the afternoon and showed no signs of slowing down."
6. "For want of a nail the kingdom was lost—that's how the catechism goes when you boil it down."
7. "The barbecue was over."
8. *"umber whunnnn"*
9. " 'Daddy, I'm tired,' the little girl in the red pants and the green blouse said fretfully."
10. "In previous years, Harold Parkette had always taken pride in his lawn."
11. "John Tell had been working at Tabori Studios just over a month when he first noticed the sneakers."
12. "Walking to school you ask me" . . .
13. "I want to tell you about the end of war, the degeneration of mankind, and the death of the messiah—an epic story deserving thousands of pages and a whole shelf of volumes, but 'you'—if there are any of you later on to read this—will have to settle for the freeze-dried version."

14. "Hapscomb's Texaco sat on US 93 just north of Arnette, a pissant four-street burg about 110 miles from Houston."
15. "Almost everyone thought the man and boy were father and son."
16. "The guy's name was Snodgrass and I could see him getting ready to do something crazy."
17. FedShip ASN/29 fell out of the sky and crashed."
18. "It's a great relief to write this down."
19. "Once, in a kingdom called Delain, there was a King with two sons."
20. "Okay, this is a science fiction joke."

III

THE NOVELS

CARRIE

Quiz 4

Carrie is the story of what can happen if you screw around with the wrong nerd in high school. Carrie White was the ultimate high school loser who was finally able to turn the tables on her tormenters and get even. I guess you could say she got a little burned up, huh?

The following questions are in three sections: "People," "Places," and "Things." The "People" section covers the characters of *Carrie*, the "Places" section deals with the locales, and the "Things" section touches on everything from dirty pillows to mass burials.

People

1. What was the name of Carrie's mother?
2. What was the name of Carrie's father?
3. Who was Carrie's gym teacher?
4. Who was the school principal?
5. Who was the assistant principal?
6. Which of Carrie's classmates conceived the "Queen of the Prom" scam?
7. What was the name of Chris Hargensen's boyfriend?
8. Which of Carrie's classmates felt guilty about the gym shower incident and so convinced her own boyfriend to take Carrie to the prom?
9. Who was King of the Prom with Carrie White?
10. Who was "Don MacLean's secret lover"?

Places

1. What was the name of Carrie's high school?
2. Where did Carrie attend grammar school?
3. Where did Margaret White work?

4. Where was Irwin Henty's farm?
5. What was Carrie White's address?
6. What was Sue Snell's address?
7. What was the name of the store from which Carrie had once stolen a forty-nine-cent finger ring?
8. Who owned Teddy's Amoco?
9. Where did Amelia Jenks live?
10. What was located at the intersection of Bellsqueeze Road and Route 6 in Chamberlain?

Things

1. What were dirtypillows?
2. Where would Carrie be "imprisoned" when she "sinned"?
3. What were the dates of the mass burials in Chamberlain after the Black Prom?
4. What kind of car did Mrs. Snell drive?
5. Name one of the two bands that played at the Ewen High Senior Prom.
6. Name one song John Swithen performed at the prom.
7. What did Chris Hargensen pour over Carrie's head at the prom?
8. What was the name of the book Sue Snell published about Carrie and the Black Prom?
9. What were the official causes of Carrie White's death?
10. What was the date of the Black Prom?

Quiz 5

'Salem's Lot concerns the travails of a quiet writer who comes back home to write a book only to find that vampires are infecting the land. Does he succumb to the vampire's seductive allure? Does he finish the book he wanted to write? Does he write a review of *De Vermis Mysteriis?* Visit the Lot and have all your questions answered!

The following questions are in three sections: "People," "Places," and "Things." The "People" section covers the characters of 'Salem's Lot, the "Places" section deals with the locales, and the "Things" section touches on everything from books to guns.

People

1. What was the name of the writer who returned to Jerusalem's Lot to do a book about the Marsten House?
2. What was the name of this writer's girlfriend?
3. What was the name of the Lot's second selectman?
4. Who owned and operated the local boardinghouse?
5. Who was having an affair with Bonnie Sawyer?
6. What was the name of the young boy who helped the writer destroy the Lot and escape?
7. Who originally owned the Marsten House?
8. What was the name of the vampire who lived in the Marsten House?
9. What was his partner's name?
10. What was the name of the 63-year-old high school English teacher who had once taught Ben Mears?

Places

1. What was the name of the Lot business owned and operated by Babs Griffen?
2. What was the name of the hill in the Lot on which the Marsten House was located?
3. What was the name of the Lot laundromat?
4. What was the name of the business owned and operated by Larry Crockett?
5. What was the name of the town in Maine where Chief Gillespie's sister lived?
6. What was the name of the Catholic church in the Lot?
7. What was the name of the business used as a front by Straker and Barlow?
8. What was the name of the small Mexican village where Mark Petrie was given holy water by Father Gracon?
9. What was the name of the street on which Eva Miller's boardinghouse was located?
10. What was the full name of 'Salem's Lot?

Things

1. What were the names of Ben Mears's three novels? (In order of appearance.)
2. What was the name of the Cumberland newspaper?
3. What was the date of Hubie Marsten's death?
4. What kind of car did Straker drive?
5. What was the title of the cartoon Father Callahan drew to accompany his monograph in *The Catholic Journal?*
6. What type of gun did Dud Rogers use to shoot rats at the dump?
7. What was the name of the dummy corporation that bought the land on which Straker and Barlow's Portland Shopping Center was to be built?
8. What type of TV did Ben's Aunt Cindy have?
9. What magazine ran an excerpt from Ben Mears's novel *Conway's Daughter?*
10. What Maine river could be seen from the back porch of Eva Miller's boardinghouse?

THE SHINING

Quiz 6

In *The Shining*, a weak and tortured man lets all manner of demons, including those real and unreal, destroy him and tear apart his family. The innocent victim of Jack's failings is ultimately his son, a helpless boy born with a gift he never asked for and does not know how to control.

The following questions are in three sections: "People," "Places," and "Things." The "People" section covers the characters of *The Shining*, the "Places" section deals with the locales, and the "Things" section touches on everything from cars to martinis.

People

1. What was the name of Jack Torrance's wife?
2. What was the name of Jack Torrance's son?
3. What was the name of Jack Torrance's son's imaginary companion?
4. Who was the manager of the Overlook Hotel?
5. Who was the head chef of the Overlook Hotel?
6. Who bought the Overlook in 1970 and later got Jack the caretaker's job?
7. What was the name of the former Overlook caretaker who went crazy and slaughtered his family in the winter of 1970–71?
8. What was the name of the Overlook bartender who gave Jack his "falling off the wagon" drink?
9. What was the name of the Overlook chambermaid who first saw the ghost of the woman in the bathtub?
10. What was the name of the student Jack cut from the debate team who later slashed Jack's tires?

Places

1. What was the closest town to the Overlook Hotel?
2. Where had Jack once taught school?
3. What was the number of the room where the dead woman lived in the bathtub?
4. Where did Hallorann work after the Overlook burned down?
5. Where did Hallorann usually spend his winters?
6. What was the name of the nursery school Danny attended before his father took the job at the Overlook?
7. Where did Jack find "the scrapbook"?
8. What was the name of the lounge in the west wing of the Overlook?
9. What room did President Nixon occupy when he visited the Overlook?
10. What was the name of the street in Colorado where the Torrances lived before Jack took the job at the Overlook?

Things

1. What precognitive gift did Hallorann share with Jack's son?
2. What were the two outdoor attractions the Overlook was most famous for?
3. What was the name of the play Jack wanted to write at the Overlook?
4. What word did Jack's son see in his dreams?
5. How many guest rooms were there in the Overlook?
6. What was the name of the short story Jack had published in *Esquire* magazine?
7. What did Al Shockley call martinis?
8. What kind of car did the Torrances drive?
9. What was the title of the book Jack considered writing about the Overlook?
10. What kind of gun did Jack own?

THE STAND

The Stand is a nightmarish vision of what would happen if 99.4 percent of the world's population was wiped out by a killer flu and the survivors were left to battle newly released powers of darkness.

The version of *The Stand* released in 1978 was not *The Stand* that Stephen King had written. In order to keep the hardcover affordable, King was asked to cut hundreds of manuscript pages from the text. The unexpurgated edition of *The Stand* was released in early 1990.

The following questions are in three sections: "People," "Places," and "Things." The "People" section covers the characters of *The Stand*, the "Places" section deals with the locales, and the "Things" section touches on everything from sex and drugs to rock and roll. (I'm only kidding about the sex.)

People

1. What was the name of the songwriter responsible for "Baby, Can You Dig Your Man?"
2. What was the name of the twenty-two-year-old deaf mute who was born in Caslin, Nebraska?
3. Who was the dark man, the man with no face?
4. What was the name of the fat high school student who was the editor of the Ogunquit High School literary magazine and who favored cowboy boots with pointed toes?
5. What was the real name of the Trashcan Man?
6. What was the name of the one-hundred-and-eight-year-old black woman who appeared in people's dreams?
7. What were the two names of Glen Bateman's dog?

8. What was the name of the guinea pig at the Atlanta Plague Center who was used to see if Stu Redman was contagious?
9. What was the name of the sixty-year-old ex-assistant professor of sociology who became part of the newly formed Ad Hoc Committee?
10. What was the name of Frannie Goldsmith and Jess Rider's son?

Places

1. Where was Hapscomb's Texaco Station?
2. Where did Harold Lauder and Frannie Goldsmith live "pre-flu"?
3. Where was the Vermont Plague Center located?
4. Where did Lloyd Henreid and Poke first meet?
5. Where was the Free Zone?
6. Where did Mother Abagail live?
7. Where was the Cheery Oil Company located?
8. What was the name of the school where Glen Bateman had taught before the flu?
9. Where was "Cibola"?
10. Where did "the stand"—the final confrontation between the forces of good and evil—take place?

Things

1. What was the name of the killer flu?
2. What was Randall Flagg's ability to see things happening elsewhere called?
3. What was the government code name for the flu?
4. What was the name of the drug Stu suggested the survivors take in order to stop their dreams about the Dark Man?
5. What was the serial number on the atomic bomb Trash brought Flagg?
6. What was the date known as "Power Day"?
7. What was the name of Larry Underwood's band?
8. What was the name of the morning phone-in radio show on KLFT in Springfield, Missouri, and who was it hosted by?
9. How did Tom Cullen spell everything?
10. What type of gun did Poke use to kill the owner of the Connie?

Quiz 8

In *The Dead Zone*, Johnny Smith awakens from a coma gifted (although he'd probably call it cursed) with the ability to foresee the future. Probably the single most significant message of the novel is that it shows us just how close we can actually come to electing psychopaths to high office.

The following questions are in three sections: "People," "Places," and "Things." The "People" section covers the characters of *The Dead Zone*, the "Places" section deals with the locales, and the "Things" section touches on everything from income tax to *Citizen Kane*.

People

1. Who was the Castle Rock Strangler?
2. What were the names of Johnny Smith's parents?
3. Who was the girl Johnny "left behind" when he entered his coma?
4. What was the name of the maniacal Presidential candidate who Johnny tried to kill in order to stop him from destroying the world?
5. What was the name of Roger Chatsworth's Vietnamese groundsman?
6. What was the name of the *Inside View* reporter who covered Johnny's story and who also appeared in the Stephen King short story "The Night Flier"?
7. What was the name of Johnny Smith's doctor?
8. Who was Sonny Elliman?
9. What was the name of the seventeen-year-old boy Johnny tutored after he came out of the coma?
10. Who were the Castle Rock Strangler's six victims?

Places

1. Where did Johnny Smith grow up?

2. Where did Sarah Bracknell grow up?
3. What was Johnny Smith's mailing address?
4. **Where did Johnny buy the rifle with which he planned to assassinate the Presidential candidate whom he knew would destroy the world if elected?**
5. What was the name of the school where John and Sarah taught?
6. What was the name of the bar owned by Bruce Carrick?
7. What was the name of the Cleaves Mills movie theater?
8. What was the name of the pond where Johnny was knocked unconscious when he was six?
9. Where was Johnny taken after the cab accident that put him in the coma?
10. What was the name of Sarah Bracknell's college dorm?

Things

1. What was the date Johnny awakened from his coma?
2. What were Johnny's first words after awakening from his coma?
3. How long was Johnny's coma?
4. What was the name of the organization that Vera Smith belonged to that believed the end of the world was imminent?
5. What did Johnny Smith call the black spots in his memory when he couldn't remember something?
6. What was the name of the supermarket tabloid that offered Johnny a job as a psychic?
7. What was the name of the Vietnamese children's game explained to Johnny by Roger Chatsworth's Vietnamese groundsman Ngo Phat?
8. What was the name of the movie John and Sarah saw on their first date?
9. What was Greg Stillson's 1975 income and income tax?
10. What was the only booth still open on the midway when Johnny and Sarah went to the Carnival on the night of Johnny's accident?

FIRESTARTER

Quiz 9

The heroine of *Firestarter* is a tot who could mentally flick her Bic anytime she wanted to. Sort of a one-note Carrie White, Charlie McGee was the offspring of two college students who participated in a Shop-sponsored drug experiment. When the Shop decided they wanted to use her as a weapon, she had to fight—first for herself, then ultimately for the survival of the world.

The following questions are in three sections: "People," "Places," and "Things." The "People" section covers the characters of *Firestarter,* the "Places" section deals with the locales, and the "Things" section touches on everything from "The Windsucker" to computer code names.

People

1. What was "Charlie" McGee's actual name?
2. What was the name of Charlie McGee's father?
3. What was the name of Charlie McGee's mother?
4. What was the name of the elderly couple who helped Charlie and her dad make a stand against the Shop?
5. Who was the head of the Shop?
6. What was the name of the Shop agent who preferred to be called either "OJ" or "The Juice"?
7. What was the name of the half-Cherokee Shop operative who stole Charlie's trust?
8. What was the name of the Shop doctor who committed suicide by sticking his hand down a garbage disposal?
9. What was the name of the doctor who headed the Shop's Lot Six experiments?

10. What was the alias Charlie's father used when he first met the elderly couple who ended up helping him and Charlie?

Places

1. What was the name of the school where Charlie's father had been an English instructor?
2. What was the name of the building where the Lot Six experiments were held?
3. Where was the Shop located?
4. Where did Rainbird lose his left eye?
5. What was the name of the faculty lounge at the college where Charlie's father had taught?
6. What was the name of the nursery school Charlie had attended and where was it located?
7. What was the name of the Bradford business owned by Shop agent Charlie Payson?
8. Where did many of the McGee's Lakeland neighbors work?
9. Where did the Shop maintain a rest-and-recreation facility?
10. On which Hawaiian island did the Shop maintain a compound?

Things

1. What month and year did Shop agents kill Charlie's mother and kidnap Charlie?
2. What was Rainbird's computer code name?
3. What was Charlie's father's legacy from the Lot Six experiments?
4. What was Irv Mander's address?
5. What was the "Bad Thing"?
6. What was Lot Six?
7. What was the Shop's real name?
8. What was Cap's computer code name?
9. What magazine did Charlie go to with her story?
10. What was "The Windsucker"?

CUJO

Quiz 10

Cujo is about a woman and a rabid dog. And a dead Pinto. And a cereal that made kids look like they were hemorrhaging. Just another of your all-American heartwarming stories about kids and animals, right?

The following questions are in three sections: "People," "Places," and "Things." The "People" section covers the characters of *Cujo*, the "Places" section deals with the locales, and the "Things" section touches on everything from Gaines Meal to screwdrivers.

People

1. Who owned Cujo?
2. What was the name of Vic Trenton's wife?
3. What was the name of their son?
4. Who was Vic Trenton's partner?
5. What was the name of the Western character developed by Ad Worx to sell cookies?
6. Who "didn't give a shit"?
7. Who was the poet/furniture refinisher Vic's wife was having an affair with?
8. What was the most famous character developed by Ad Worx for the Sharp cereal account?
9. What was the name of the custodian in Vic's building?
10. Who was "Adam Swallow"?

Places

1. Where did Cujo live?
2. Where did the Breakstones live?
3. Where did Charity Camber's sister Holly live?

4. What was the name of the only tavern in Castle Rock?
5. What was the name of the Camber place and on what road was it located?
6. Name two cities where Red Razberry Zingers were successfully test marketed.
7. In what town did Cujo's vet have his practice?
8. What was the House of Lights, Inc.?
9. Where did Ad Worx shoot the Book Folks ad spots?
10. Where did Yancey Harrington live?

Things

1. What was the name of Vic and Roger's agency?
2. What month and year was Gary Pervier discharged from the service?
3. What brands of dog food did Cujo eat?
4. What was the kind of car in which Donna was trapped by Cujo?
5. What were the "Monster Words"?
6. What did the mole just above Donna Trenton's pubic hair look like?
7. What was Tad Trenton's nickname?
8. What was the Trentons's address?
9. What was Gary Pervier's screwdriver recipe?
10. Name one of the cereals produced by the Sharp company.

Quiz 11

"Christine." The name reminds us of so many sweet things: choking to death, motor oil, and exhaust fumes. Stephen King's great American car and rock 'n' roll novel reminds us *never* to neglect our rolling stock.

The following questions are in three sections: "People," "Places," and "Things." The "People" section covers the characters of *Christine*, the "Places" section deals with the locales, and the "Things" section touches on everything from cars to more cars (with a UPS truck thrown in for good measure).

People

1. Who was "Arnie's first love . . . his only true love"?
2. What was the name of the creep who hated Arnie and ended up trashing Christine?
3. Who was Arnie's girlfriend?
4. Who was Arnie's best friend?
5. What was the name of the police officer who questioned Michael Cunningham about Arnie's possible connection to Moochie Welch's death?
6. Who sold Christine to Arnie?
7. What was the name of the hitchhiker who saved Leigh's life as she was choking in Christine?
8. Who was the parking lot attendant at the airport where Arnie parked Christine?
9. Who owned the repair shop where Arnie garaged Christine?
10. Who did Dennis take to see *Grease?*

Places

1. Where does *Christine* take place?
2. Where did Dennis and Arnie go to high school?
3. What place was a "crazy automotive Disneyland"?
4. Where did Leigh Cabot move after marrying the IBM rep Ackerman?
5. What was the former name of JFK Drive?
6. On what street did the Cunninghams live?
7. In what town had George LeBay taught English for almost forty years?
8. Where was the university at which Regina and Michael Cunningham taught?
9. What college did Leigh Cabot and Dennis Guilder attend?
10. What was the name of the lower-class neighborhood near Libertyville?

Things

1. What was the color, year, make, and model of Christine?
2. What kind of car did Buddy Repperton drive?
3. What kind of car did Richie Trelawney drive?
4. What kind of car did Will Darnell drive?
5. What kind of car did Dennis Guilder drive?
6. What kind of car did Sandy Galton drive?
7. What kind of car did Gabbs drive?
8. What kind of car did Roland LeBay buy the year after he got married?
9. What was Christine's mileage the day Arnie bought her?
10. What hit and killed Dennis's cat Captain Beefheart?

PET SEMATARY

Quiz 12

Pet Sematary shows us what happens when man plays God. The novel tells the tale of a young doctor given the chance to "overrule" death . . . and God. *Pet Sematary* was made into a movie and released in April of 1989. It was directed by Mary Lambert (the film *Siesta*, and Madonna's *Like a Virgin*, *Material Girl*, and *Like a Prayer* videos) and starred Fred Gwynne and Denise Crosby.

The following questions are in three sections: "People," "Places," and "Things." The "People" section covers the characters of *Pet Sematary*, the "Places" section deals with the locales, and the "Things" section touches on everything from kites to caskets.

People

1. What was the name of Louis Creed's wife?
2. What were the names of the Creed children?
3. What was the name of the 83-year-old man who lived across the street from the Creeds?
4. Who babysat for the Creed children?
5. What was the name of Louis Creed's father-in-law?
6. What was the name of Louis Creed's physician's assistant?
7. What was the name of the dying boy who told Louis Creed "It's not the real cemetery"?
8. What was the name of the tribe that had laid claim to the state land which abutted the Creeds's property?
9. What was the name of the Creeds's cat?
10. Who neutered the Creeds's cat?

Places

1. What was the name of the university's cafeteria?
2. What was the name of the woods behind Louis Creed's house?
3. What was the name of the swamp on the edge of the deadfall?
4. What was the name of Ellie's school in Chicago?
5. Where did the Goldmans stay when they came to Maine for their grandson's funeral?
6. What was the name of the Chinese restaurant near the Eastern Maine Medical Center?
7. What was the name of the company that manufactured Gage's coffin?
8. Where were the Crandalls's burial plots located?
9. Where was Timmy Baterman's body brought?
10. What was the name of the mortuary that claimed Victor Pascow's body and handled Norma Crandall's funeral?

Things

1. What kind of car did Louis Creed drive?
2. What was the name of Louis Creed's kite?
3. What was the date of Gage Creed's funeral?
4. What was the model casket Louis picked out for his son?
5. What was D-day?
6. What was "The Front file"?
7. What kind of cigarettes did Jud Crandall smoke?
8. What did Mr. and Mrs. Goldman give to the Creeds as a wedding gift?
9. How did Ellie pronounce Santa?
10. What did Louis have to climb over to get to the Micmac Burying Ground?

THE TALISMAN

Quiz 13

Stephen King's only collaborative effort to date is *The Talisman*. He and Peter Straub worked together on this epic quest that owes more than a nod to Mark Twain and J.R.R. Tolkien. Supposedly, Steven Spielberg has bought the film rights, but so far, nothing's happened with the project. We've heard that Spielberg plans to change either Jack's or Richard's character to a female character. Casting this role, and this film, ought to be *verrrry* interesting! (Can't you see Jack Nicholson as Sunlight Gardener?)

The following questions are in three sections: "People," "Places," and "Things." The "People" section covers the characters of *The Talisman*, the "Places" section deals with the locales in the story, and the "Things" section touches on everything from weapons to mottos.

People

1. What was the name of Jack Sawyer's mother?
2. What was the name of the black man Jack met in New Hampshire?
3. What was the name of Jack's father?
4. What was the name of Jack's father's evil business partner?
5. Who was Jack's best friend?
6. Who was Jack's Twinner?
7. What was the name of the half-boy/half-wolf Jack met in the Territories?
8. What was the name of the old man who lived in the depot on the edge of the Blasted Lands?
9. Who owned the Oatley Tap?
10. Who was the director of the Sunlight Home?

Places

1. What was the name of the hotel in New Hampshire where Jack and his mother moved to from New York?
2. Where was the black hotel?
3. What was the name of the land where our world's Twinners lived?
4. What was the name of the school Richard Sloat attended?
5. What was the name of the tunnel Jack had to cross in order to get to Oatley?
6. What lands did Jack and Richard have to cross to get to the black hotel?
7. Where did the talisman reside?
8. What was the name of the amusement park where Speedy worked?
9. Where did Queen Laura DeLoessian lie on her deathbed, awaiting Jack's "rescue"?
10. Where was Far Field?

Things

1. What was the name of the Territories' sacred book?
2. What was the month Jack and his mother moved to New Hampshire?
3. What was Jack's mother's last film role?
4. What did Speedy give Jack (in addition to the magic juice) to help him in his travels?
5. What did Speedy's gift transform into after Jack flipped?
6. What was Wolf's "motto"?
7. What was the circumference of the Talisman?
8. What killed Tommy Woodbine?
9. What did Captain Farren give Jack, telling him he'd know what to do with it when the time came?
10. What kind of weapons did Jack and Richard find on Morgan's train?

CYCLE OF THE WEREWOLF

Quiz 14

Tell the truth: You knew who the Werewolf was all along didn't you?!

Cycle of the Werewolf originally began as a calendar idea. Chris Zavisa approached King with the idea of an illustrated calendar, with King writing a short vignette for each month of the year. The thing began to grow, and *Cycle of the Werewolf* was the result.

Cycle of the Werewolf was made into the film *Silver Bullet.*

The following questions are in three sections: "People," "Places," and "Things." The "People" section covers the characters of *Cycle of the Werewolf*, the "Places" section deals with the locales, and the "Things" section touches on everything from beer to wheelchairs.

People

1. Who was the werewolf?
2. Who was the 10-year-old crippled kid who discovered the werewolf's identity?
3. Who was the kid's favorite uncle?
4. Who was the werewolf's January—and first—victim?
5. Who was the werewolf's November victim?
6. Who owned the eleven pigs that were the werewolf's September victims?
7. Who melted down Marty's confirmation spoon to make two silver bullets?
8. Who is the weatherman on "The Today Show"?
9. Who owned Stan's Barber Shop?
10. Who was the Grace Baptist Church's head deacon?

Places

1. In what town was *Cycle of the Werewolf* set?
2. Where was Arnie Westrum killed by the werewolf?
3. On what street did Willie Harrington live?
4. What was the name of the hayfield owned by Old Man Hague?
5. What was the name of the diner on Main Street?
6. What was the name of the park where they usually held the fireworks display?
7. Where was Donna Lee Sturmfuller taken after her husband Milt beat her for leaving some dried egg on his dish?
8. What was the name of the business run by Stella Randolph?
9. What was the name of the market in town?
10. Where did Constable Neary and his wife Joan live?

Things

1. What was the "Great Spring Drunk"?
2. What was the name of the sermon the Reverend Lowe dreamed he gave on Homecoming Sunday?
3. What was the Reverend Lowe's address?
4. How did Marty Coslaw get around?
5. What brand of cigarettes did Arnie Westrum smoke?
6. What was the "Big Pal" voice?
7. What kind of kite did Brady Kincaid have?
8. What was the name of the football team Lander Neary played on when he was in high school?
9. Who wrote the note to the werewolf that said "I know who you are"?
10. How was the werewolf killed?

IT

Quiz 15

It is my single favorite Stephen King novel of all time, and it is also the novel I consider his best work. *It* has it all, and I don't think describing the novel as a "magnum opus" is an overstatement. It is quintessential King—and quintessential horror—and yet there are moments of such sublime tenderness in the story that many times I found myself absolutely lost in the forest of King's words. A magnificent novel that stands as an American classic.

The following questions are in three sections: "People," "Places," and "Things." The "People" section covers the characters of *It*, the "Places" section deals with the locales, and the "Things" section touches on everything from bikes to a radio station.

People

1. Who was Bob Gray?
2. What was the name of the only Loser to remain in Derry?
3. What was the name of the only female Loser?
4. What was the name of the Loser who committed suicide rather than return to Derry and once again face It?
5. What was the name of the cook at the Black Spot?
6. What was the name of the pseudo-asthmatic Loser?
7. What was the name of the Loser who did "Voices"?
8. What was the name of the Loser who grew up to be a novelist?
9. Who was the fat Loser?
10. What were the names of the three creeps who tormented the Losers as kids?

Places

1. Where did the Losers build the dam?
2. Where were two of the Losers attacked by the Teenage Werewolf?
3. From where did the two dead kids come who chased Stan while he was out birdwatching?
4. Where did Mike Hanlon work?
5. What was the name of the Chinese restaurant where the Losers had their first reunion?
6. What was the name of the bar where Eddie King was chopped to pieces with an axe by Claude Heroux?
7. What was the name of the "nightclub" at the Derry Army Air Corps Base that burned down in 1930?
8. What was the name of the park in Bangor where Franklin D'Cruz was caught after raping more than fifty women?
9. What was the name of the gay bar in Derry that was decorated with stuffed birds?
10. Where did It live?

Things

1. What was on the bottom shelf of Eddie Kaspbrak's medicine chest?
2. What was the name of Bill's bike?
3. What was the name of Bill Denbrough's first published short story, and in what magazine was it published?
4. What was the name of "Bangor's AM stereo rocker"?
5. What was Ben Hanscom's Nebraska address?
6. What did people usually see floating around after a manifestation by It?
7. What was the name of the Ritual that allowed Bill to triumph over It?
8. What was the name of Beverly Rogan's clothing company?
9. What was Richie Tozier's listeners' all-time favorite character?
10. Which of Georgie Denbrough's arms did It rip off when Georgie reached into the sewer drain?

THE EYES OF THE DRAGON

Quiz 16

The Eyes of the Dragon was written by King for his daughter Naomi after she complained that she didn't like reading his horror novels. She loved *Eyes*, and so did King's readers. It's a wondrous fable complete with a dragon, a wizard, Kings, a castle, spells, and a Tolkien-esque charm that carries you along effortlessly.

The following questions are in three sections: "People," "Places," and "Things." The "People" section covers the characters of *The Eyes of the Dragon*, the "Places" section deals with the locales, and the "Things" section touches on everything from Foe-Hammer to a somewhat strange "pet."

People

1. Who was the King of Delain?
2. Who was falsely accused of killing the King?
3. What was the name of the King's wife, the mother of his sons?
4. What was the name of the King's younger son?
5. What was the name of the King's magician?
6. What was the name of the dragon killed by the King?
7. Who was Peter's best friend?
8. What was the name of Peter's horse?
9. Who built Sasha's dollhouse?
10. Who was the Chief Warder of the Needle?

Places

1. Where did Dragon Sand come from?
2. Where did Deadly Clawfoot grow?

3. Where was the trial held for the accused murderer of the King?
4. Where was the book of spells written?
5. What was the name of the barony where Roland's wife had come from?
6. Where did Flagg come from?
7. What was the lowest point in the castle?
8. Where did Flagg hide to spy on the King?
9. What was the name of the "very old Kingdom" where the story takes place?
10. Where did Peter compete in the Bowmanship Classes against Lord Towson's son?

Things

1. What was the name of the book written by the madman Alhazred?
2. What did Flagg keep as a pet?
3. What was "Tom's Black Tax"?
4. How long did it take for Peter's beard to grow to the middle of his chest?
5. What did Roland eat after he killed the dragon?
6. What was Foe-Hammer?
7. How did Dennis gain entrance to the east wing of the castle?
8. Where did Flagg keep his poison?
9. What did Peter do to his napkins every day?
10. What did Peter find beneath the Loose Stone in the Needle?

MISERY

Quiz 17

Misery is a nasty novel that was originally supposed to be a "Richard Bachman" book. It tells a dark story of mutual parasitism and contains an amputation scene guaranteed to "linger" in your memory for a long, long time. Interestingly, *Misery*, which does not contain a single vampire, haunted house, or zombie, is ranked by many readers as their favorite King novel of all time. It makes sense: All the monsters in the world can't hold a candle to the twisted psyche of the scariest creature of all: the human monster.

The following questions are in three sections: "People," "Places," and "Things." The "People" section covers the characters of *Misery*, the "Places" section deals with the locales, and the "Things" section touches on everything from pills to publishers.

People

1. What was the name of the psychotic nurse who kidnapped the writer?
2. What was the name of the writer responsible for the Misery novels?
3. What was Misery's last name?
4. What was the name of the writer's father?
5. What was the name of the writer's agent?
6. What was the name of the character in the writer's first non-Misery novel who "has no nobility"?
7. What was the name of the nurse's ex-husband?
8. What were the names of the two officers who carried the writer from the nurse's house?
9. What was the name of the writer's post-captivity editor?

10. Who wrote the article entitled "Head Maternity Nurse Questioned on Infant Deaths"?

Places

1. What was the name of the store the nurse checked for the writer's paperbacks?
2. What was the name of the beach the writer remembered from his childhood?
3. What was the name of the hospital in Harrisburg, Pennsylvania, where the nurse had once worked?
4. What was the name of the hospital where much of the first Misery book had been set?
5. What was the name of the day-care center where the writer had played "Can You?" as a child?
6. Where did the writer complete the manuscript of his first non-Misery novel?
7. Where was Misery's Parlor?
8. What hospital cared for the writer after his captivity?
9. Where did the writer live after his captivity?
10. Where did Eddie Desmond find the skunk?

Things

1. What did the writer's father give to his son on his fourteenth birthday?
2. On the day of the storm, which of the writer's novels had the nurse been hoping was out in paperback?
3. What kind of car had the writer been driving when he had the accident?
4. What was the name of the novel the writer thought may win him an American Book Award?
5. What was the name of the novel the nurse forced the writer to write for her?
6. What did the nurse use to "hobble" the writer, and what did she take from him?
7. What was the name of the writer's pain medication?
8. How much did the writer's editor think they could get for a nonfiction account of the writer's captivity?

9. What was the name of the publishing company that published the novel the writer was forced to write while being held captive?

10. What was the brand of typewriter the writer hurled at the nurse?

THE TOMMYKNOCKERS

Quiz 18

The Tommyknockers is a science fiction horror novel that asks the question "Do you *really* want to know what's buried in your backyard?" King has referred to this tale as a "gadget" novel, and that's a very apt description. The story concerns a writer who unknowingly unleashes the powers of the Tommyknockers on her small Maine town. It is a complex nightmare and a disturbing reminder of the powers we carelessly screw around with every single day.

The following questions are in three sections: "People," "Places," and "Things." The "People" section covers the characters of *The Tommyknockers*, the "Places" section deals with the locales, and the "Things" section touches on everything from books to magic tricks.

People

1. What was the name of Bobbi's alcoholic poet friend?
2. What was the name of Bobbi Anderson's beagle?
3. What was the name of Bobbi's bitch sister?
4. What was the name of Bobbi's mailman?
5. What was the name of the poet whose family had made a lot of money in the textile business?
6. Who did Bobbi's poet friend meet on a beach after the worst drinking jag of his life?
7. What was the name of the little boy who disappeared during a magic trick performed by his brother?
8. What was the name of the local lawyer who had a doll collection?

9. What was the name of the Bangor reporter who talked to John Leandro over beers in the Bounty Tavern?
10. Who jumped into Hazel McCready's dry well?

Places

1. What was the name of the town where Bobbi found the spaceship?
2. What was Bobbi's property known as around town?
3. What was the name of the street in New York where Bobbi had "first smelled sage"?
4. Where was Ev Hillman held prisoner in a shower cabinet with a coaxial cable running out of his right eye?
5. What was the name of the beach where Bobbi's poet friend met the young boy?
6. Where did the little boy who disappeared during the magic trick go?
7. After the fire, where were the town's twenty-six remaining Tommyknockers taken?
8. Where did Ruth McCausland die?
9. Where did Bobbi Anderson die?
10. Where did Gard die?

Things

1. What was the date Bobbi Anderson "stumbled over her destiny"?
2. What was the name of Bobbi's first western novel, and what year was it published?
3. What was the name of Jim Gardener's first book of poetry?
4. After Bobbi's modifications, what did her water heater use as a power source?
5. What three magic tricks did Hilly Brown perform before his Grand Finale, the Disappearing Little Brother?
6. What was the name of the novel Bobbi wrote telepathically?
7. What was the name of the bar owned and operated by Hiram Cooder?

8. What prevented Bobbi from being able to read her poet friend's thoughts?
9. What magazine was 'Becka Paulson reading just before she electrocuted her husband?
10. What was the name of the newspaper David Bright wrote for?

THE DARK HALF

Dark indeed is *The Dark Half*. It's a mesmerizing, violent story of writer Thad Beaumont who creates a pseudonym that literally takes on a life of its own. In the Author's Note at the beginning of the book, Stephen King thanks the late Richard Bachman, acknowledging that *The Dark Half* "could not have been written without him." I read the book in eight hours in a feverish, almost hypnotic state, and realized when I was finished that I had been through the quintessential "Stephen King Experience": The story had become my world for that brief time spent buried in the book's pages.

The following questions are in three sections: "People," "Places," and "Things." The "People" section covers the characters of *The Dark Half*, the "Places" section deals with the locales, and the "Things" section touches on everything from books to birds.

People

1. What was the name of Thad Beaumont's "dark half"?
2. What was the name of the "hero" Beaumont created for his pseudonymous line of novels?
3. What was the name of Thad's wife?
4. What were the names of the Beaumont twins?
5. What was the name of Thad Beaumont's literary agent?
6. What was the name of the first victim of Thad's dark half?
7. What was the name of the sheriff who witnessed the demise of Thad's dark half?
8. What was the name of the doctor who operated on Thad as a child?

9. What was the name of the absentminded professor who lent Thad his car?
10. Who stored pot in his barn?

Places

1. Where was Thad Beaumont born and raised?
2. According to the publishing company's bio sheet, where was Thad's dark half born?
3. What was the name of the Mississippi town where Thad's dark half acquired his Southern accent?
4. Henry Payton was based at what Maine State Police Barracks?
5. Where was Thad's dark half "buried"?
6. Where did Hugh Pritchard move to after he retired?
7. Where was Frederick Clawson murdered?
8. What was the name of the road on which the Beaumont summer house was located?
9. Where did all rail service terminate?
10. Where did Thad's dark half go?

Things

1. What were the titles of Thad Beaumont's two "Beaumont" novels?
2. What was the name of the novel Thad was working on when his dark half "came back from the dead"?
3. What were the titles of Thad Beaumont's four pseudonymous novels?
4. What were psychopomps?
5. Before his childhood brain surgery, what did Thad hear in his head?
6. What was the weapon of choice for Thad's dark half?
7. What was the brand of pencil Thad used to write his pseudonymous novels?
8. What was the name of the final attempted collaboration between Thad and his dark half?
9. What was written on the wall above Frederick Clawson's dead body?
10. What kind of car did Thad's dark half drive and what did the bumper sticker on it say?

IV

THE SHORTER COLLECTED WORKS

The following questions are from the short story "Heritage"

NIGHT SHIFT
"Jerusalem's Lot"

Quiz 20

The following questions are from the short story "Jerusalem's Lot" from the collection *Night Shift*.

1. What was the date of the first letter Charles Boone wrote after arriving at his ancestral home?
2. To whom was the letter addressed, and where was the addressee?
3. What was the name of Charles Boone's ancestral home?
4. How many rooms did the house have?
5. What was the name of Charles Boone's manservant?
6. What was the name of Charles Boone's deceased wife?
7. What was the name of the woman Charles brought in to clean the house?
8. What was the name of the book Charles found in the abandoned Jerusalem's Lot church?
9. What type of cypher did Robert Boone use to encode his diary?
10. What was the name of the final descendant of the Boone line—the man who took occupancy of the house in 1971?

NIGHT SHIFT
"Graveyard Shift"

Quiz 21

The following questions are from the short story "Grave-yard Shift" from the collection *Night Shift*.

1. What was the name of the mill foreman?
2. Where was the mill located?
3. When did Hall start working at the mill?
4. What machine did Hall operate?
5. Who sent the orders down to Hall?
6. What job did Hall agree to do on the Fourth of July?
7. What was beneath the mill's subbasement?
8. When was the mill built?
9. What creature did Hall and Warwick find in the mill's basement?
10. Who went looking for Hall and Warwick?

Quiz 22

The following questions are from the short story "Night Surf" from the collection *Night Shift*.

1. What was the official name of the killer flu?
2. What was the name of the kid who had the radio and who was well-to-do before the flu?
3. What was the name of the guy the kids burned on the beach?
4. What was the name of the narrator of the story?
5. What was the name of the DJ on WDOPE?
6. What was the name of the girl who was getting fat and who was wearing cranberry bellbottoms?
7. What did the kids call the flu?
8. Who actually lit the pyre of the guy they burned on the beach?
9. What sickness supposedly made a person immune to the killer flu?
10. Where did Susie and Bernie meet Needles?

Quiz 23

The following questions are from the short story "I Am the Doorway" from the collection *Night Shift*.

1. Who was "the doorway"?
2. What was the name of the project to "find something" out there?
3. Who was the project's "whiz kid"?
4. What was the name of the doorway's friend who sold driftwood sculptures?
5. Who was the doorway's partner on the trip during which he was "invaded"?
6. What was their destination?
7. What was the DESA and what happened to it?
8. Who was the Navy Department investigator who checked on the doorway once a year?
9. Who was the doorway's doctor?
10. Before the doorway shot himself, where had he grown eyes?

NIGHT SHIFT
"The Mangler"

Quiz 24

The following questions are from the short story "The Mangler" from the collection *Night Shift*.

1. What was the name of the laundry where the mangler lived?
2. Who owned the laundry?
3. What was the mangler?
4. What was the name of the first woman killed by the machine?
5. What was the name of the first officer to report to the scene after her death?
6. What was the name of his college professor friend who learned how to summon demons?
7. What were some of the elements needed to summon a demon?
8. Who was the state inspector who investigated the accident?
9. Who was the laundry foreman?
10. Whose blood started the chain of events that would culminate with the mangler being possessed?

Quiz 25

The following questions are from the short story "The Boogeyman" from the collection *Night Shift*.

1. What was the name of Lester Billings's psychiatrist?
2. Where did Billings live?
3. What was the name of the psychiatrist's nurse?
4. What were the names of Billings's kids?
5. When did they die?
6. Who did Shirl look like?
7. What was the name of Billings's wife?
8. What was the official cause of Billings's daughter's death?
9. How often did the psychiatrist want to see Billings?
10. Who was the boogeyman?

NIGHT SHIFT
"Gray Matter"

Quiz 26

The following questions are from the short story "Gray Matter" from the collection *Night Shift*.

1. What was the name of the store where the guys hung out during the blizzard?
2. Who owned the store?
3. What was the name of the guy who drank the bad beer?
4. What was the name of his son?
5. What was the name of the gray matter guy's doctor?
6. What was the brand of beer that "changed" our friend into "gray matter"?
7. What was the name of the guy who worked for the Bangor Public Works Department and once saw a spider the size of a dog in a sewer?
8. What was the name of the narrator's dog that had been hit by a car?
9. What was the name of the street where "Mr. Gray Matter" lived?
10. How long did it take Richie to drink twenty two-bit glasses of beer in Wally's Spa?

NIGHT SHIFT
"Battleground"

Quiz 27

The following questions are from the short story "Battleground" from the collection *Night Shift*.

1. Who called John Renshaw with the job for the Organization?
2. What was Renshaw's minimum fee?
3. Who had been Renshaw's target?
4. What was the name of his victim's company?
5. Who sent Renshaw the package containing the G.I. Joe Vietnam Footlocker?
6. What were the contents of the footlocker stenciled on the box?
7. What kind of gun did Renshaw use?
8. What did the note say that the soldiers sent Renshaw?
9. Who saw the nuclear flash when the soldiers nuked Renshaw?
10. What were the special added attractions included in the footlocker (For a Limited Time Only)?

NIGHT SHIFT
"Trucks"

Quiz 28

The following questions are from the short story "Trucks" from the collection *Night Shift*.

1. What was the name of the salesman trapped in the truck stop?
2. What was the name of the truck stop?
3. What kind of car did the narrator own?
4. What was the name of the kid in the Fury?
5. Where had he been heading?
6. How did the trucks signal the people in the truck stop that they wanted gas?
7. What song did the kid from the Fury play on the jukebox?
8. How was the trucker who bolted out of the truck stop killed?
9. What kind of gas did the truck stop carry?
10. What was the narrator referring to when he thought "I wish I could believe there are people in them"?

NIGHT SHIFT
"Sometimes They Come Back"

The following questions are from the short story "Sometimes They Come Back" from the collection *Night Shift*.

1. What was the name of Jim Norman's wife?
2. What was the name of the school where Jim was hired as an English teacher?
3. Who interviewed Jim for the job?
4. Who was the head of the English Department?
5. What was the name of Jim's dead brother?
6. What were the names of the guys who killed Jim's brother?
7. What kind of car did the three killers drive and what was written on the side of the car?
8. What was the title of the book Jim used to raise the spirit of his dead brother?
9. What body parts did Jim offer in the summoning of the demons ritual?
10. What were the last words Jim's brother said to him before his spirit vanished?

NIGHT SHIFT
"Strawberry Spring"

Quiz 30

The following questions are from the short story "Strawberry Spring" from the collection *Night Shift*.

1. On what date did the "strawberry spring" begin?
2. Where does the story take place?
3. Who was Springheel Jack's first victim?
4. What was the name of the student who found Jack's first victim?
5. How was she killed?
6. What was the name of the victim who was found without her head?
7. Where was Adelle Parkins found?
8. Who was arrested for the murder of Adelle Parkins?
9. Who was killed after Adelle Parkins?
10. Who was Springheel Jack?

NIGHT SHIFT
"The Ledge"

Quiz 31

The following questions are from the short story "The Ledge" from the collection *Night Shift*.

1. Who bet Stan Norris he couldn't walk around the building on the ledge?
2. How high up was the ledge?
3. Who was Stan Norris having an affair with?
4. What was planted in the trunk of Stan Norris's car?
5. What were the terms of the wager Stan was forced to make?
6. What was the name of the guy who was waiting for a call telling him what to do with the contents of Stan's trunk?
7. How wide was the ledge?
8. What time did Stan make it back to the balcony, after having successfully made it all the way around the building?
9. Norris won the money, his freedom, and Marcia. But where was Marcia?
10. How did Norris get even?

NIGHT SHIFT
"The Lawnmower Man"

Quiz 32

The following questions are from the short story "The Lawnmower Man" from the collection *Night Shift*.

1. What kind of lawnmower did Harold Parkette own?
2. What was the name of Harold's wife?
3. What happened to the Smith's cat?
4. How old was Jenny Smith?
5. When would Jenny Smith hide in Harold's lawn?
6. What company did Harold call to cut his lawn?
7. What was their phone number?
8. What was the name of the company Harold had once bought shares in?
9. What was Harold's address?
10. Who was the bartender at the Goldfish Bowl?

NIGHT SHIFT
"Quitters, Inc."

Quiz 33

The following questions are from the short story "Quitters, Inc." from the collection *Night Shift*.

1. Who introduced Dick Morrison to Quitters, Inc.?
2. What was Dick Morrison's address?
3. What was the name of Dick's mentally retarded son?
4. What was the name of the Quitters, Inc. counselor who was in charge of Dick's case?
5. What was the name of Dick's wife?
6. What was the name of the businessman who endowed Quitters, Inc. with its funding?
7. What was step ten in the Quitters, Inc. program?
8. What Quitters, Inc. slogan was on their business cards?
9. What was the amount of Dick Morrison's Quitters, Inc. bill?
10. What was the punishment for a client exceeding his maximum weight?

NIGHT SHIFT
"I Know What You Need"

Quiz 34

The following questions are from the short story "I Know What You Need" from the collection *Night Shift*.

1. What was the first thing Ed Hamner told Elizabeth she needed?
2. What was the name of Elizabeth's roommate?
3. What was the name of Elizabeth's sociology professor?
4. What minimum score did Elizabeth need on her final in order to keep her scholarship?
5. Who was Tony Lombard?
6. What did Elizabeth and Ed win at the Homecoming Nostalgia Dance?
7. What was Elizabeth's mother's nickname?
8. What books did Elizabeth find in the locked box in Ed's room?
9. Name three of the six things Elizabeth found inside the "Bridgeport Candy Co." tin box in Ed's room.
10. Who did Mrs. Hamner think was "the devil's henchman"?

NIGHT SHIFT
"Children of the Corn"

Quiz 35

The following questions are from the short story "Children of the Corn" from the collection *Night Shift*.

1. What was the name of Burt Robeson's wife?
2. What position had Burt held while serving in Vietnam?
3. Where did Burt and his wife bring the body of the boy they hit on Route 17?
4. Who was "The Singing Marvel"?
5. How much was the strawberry rhubarb pie in the Gatlin Bar and Grill?
6. What was the July 24, 1976 sermon at the Grace Baptist Church?
7. What was Sandra Clawson's "new" name?
8. What was playing at the Bijou Theater?
9. What was the name of the Seer?
10. Whose child was Ruth carrying?

"The Last Rung on the Ladder"

Quiz 36

The following questions are from the short story "The Last Rung on the Ladder" from the collection *Night Shift*.

1. What was the name of Larry's sister?
2. How was the last letter his sister ever wrote him addressed?
3. What was the name of Larry's ex-wife?
4. Where did Larry's family grow up?
5. What was Larry's occupation?
6. How many rungs were on the ladder?
7. How high off the barn floor was the plank Larry and his sister used to jump off?
8. What was the name of the doctor who set Larry's sister's broken ankle?
9. What did the headline read that reported Larry's sister's death?
10. What was the one sentence from his sister that was "maybe the only thing that would have brought [Larry] on the run"?

Night Shift
"The Man Who Loved Flowers"

Quiz 37

The following questions are from the short story "The Man Who Loved Flowers" from the collection *Night Shift*.

1. What month and year was "the man who loved flowers" out walking?
2. What town was he in?
3. What color were his eyes?
4. What was the name of the girl he once brought presents?
5. What was her favorite fruit?
6. How long had she been dead?
7. Where did he find the girl in the sailor blouse?
8. How did he kill the girl in the sailor blouse?
9. How many others had he killed?
10. What was the name of "the man who loved flowers"?

Quiz 38

The following questions are from the short story "One for the Road" from the collection *Night Shift*.

1. Who owned Tookey's Bar?
2. Who was the town's snowplow driver?
3. What was the name of the story's narrator?
4. What was the name of the guy who got lost in the blizzard?
5. Where was he from?
6. What was the name of his wife?
7. What was the name of his daughter?
8. Where did he leave them when he went to get help?
9. Who once got drunk, went into the Lot at night, and was never seen again?
10. What happened to the wife and daughter?

NIGHT SHIFT
"The Woman in the Room"

Quiz 39

The following questions are from the short story "The Woman in the Room" from the collection *Night Shift*.

1. What hospital was John's mother in?
2. What room was she in?
3. What was the name of John's brother?
4. What operation was performed on John's mother in an attempt to lessen her pain?
5. What illness was killing John's mother?
6. Where did John buy the beer he used to anesthetize himself for his visits to his mother?
7. How many miles was it from John's house to the hospital?
8. Where did John's brother live?
9. How tall was the doctor who performed the surgery on John's mother?
10. How did John's mother die?

DIFFERENT SEASONS
"Rita Hayworth and Shawshank Redemption"

Quiz 40

The following questions are from the novella "Rita Hayworth and Shawshank Redemption" from the collection *Different Seasons*.

1. Who was Shawshank's "Neiman-Marcus"?
2. What was the name of the banker convicted of murder who asked for a Rita Hayworth poster in 1949?
3. What was the name of Linda Dufresne's lover?
4. What was the name of Shawshank's warden?
5. Who lived in Cell 14 of Cellblock 5?
6. What was the name of the Mexican town twenty miles from Playa Azul?
7. What was the name of the program instituted by the warden in which inmates worked outside the prison?
8. On what date did Red receive a blank postcard from McNary, Texas?
9. What month and year was the license-plate factory roof re-tarred?
10. What year did the Rita Hayworth poster admirer escape from Shawshank?

DIFFERENT SEASONS
"Apt Pupil"

Quiz 41

The following questions are from the novella "Apt Pupil" from the collection *Different Seasons*.

1. What was the alias Kurt Dussander used in America after the war?
2. Who discovered Dussander's real identity?
3. What was the name of the man who set up a stock portfolio for Dussander?
4. What was Harold Pegler's nickname?
5. What was the name of the man who broke his back, ended up in the same intensive care room as Dussander, and realized he remembered him from the death camps?
6. Where did the boy who discovered Dussander's identity buy the old man an SS uniform?
7. Where was Dussander stationed as commandant during the war?
8. What was Pegasus?
9. What kind of weapon did Todd use for his highway killing spree?
10. How did Dussander die?

DIFFERENT SEASONS
"The Body"

Quiz 42

The following questions are from the novella "The Body" from the collection *Different Seasons*.

1. Who were the boys who set out on the hunt for "the body"?
2. Who was "the body"?
3. Who was the Castle Rock dumpkeeper?
4. What was the name of his dog?
5. What was Chico's real name?
6. Who was the Mayor of Gretna?
7. What river did the boys have to cross to complete their journey?
8. What happened when the boys went swimming in the beaver pond during their journey?
9. Who was the toughest guy in Castle Rock?
10. Who did the boys consider "the meanest bitch God had ever set down on the earth"?

DIFFERENT SEASONS
"The Breathing Method"

The following questions are from the novella "The Breathing Method" from the collection *Different Seasons*.

1. What was the name of the club's butler?
2. What was the name of the doctor who told the story of the Breathing Method?
3. What was the name of the doctor's Breathing Method patient?
4. What was the club's address?
5. What was the name of the guest who visited the club the night the story of the Breathing Method was told?
6. What was the date this particular storytelling session took place?
7. What was the name of Edward Gray Seville's first novel?
8. What was the legend engraved on the stone above the fireplace at the club?
9. What was the Breathing Method?
10. Who was George Waterhouse?

Quiz 44

The following questions are from the novella "The Mist" from the collection *Skeleton Crew*.

1. Where did the Draytons live?
2. What was the name of Dave Drayton's wife?
3. What was the name of Dave Drayton's son?
4. What was the name of the Draytons's neighbor who had once lost a boundary dispute to the Draytons?
5. What was the name of the supermarket where everyone was trapped by the mist?
6. What was the name of the religious fanatic who owned the antique shop?
7. What was the name of the old man who offered to make a run for the shotgun in the trunk of his car?
8. Where did Drayton write the story of what happened after the storm?
9. What was in the mist?
10. Where did Drayton and his group head for, and what word did it sound like?

SKELETON CREW
"Here There Be Tygers"

Quiz 45

The following questions are from the short story "Here There Be Tygers" from the collection *Skeleton Crew*.

1. Who needed to go to the bathroom?
2. What grade was he in?
3. What was the name of his teacher?
4. Name one of his classmates.
5. What third grade teacher was shaped like "a Moorish pillow"?
6. What kind of car did Miss Kinney's boyfriend drive?
7. What was the name of the paper towel dispenser in the school lavatory?
8. What downtown theatre had a stinky bathroom?
9. What was the name of one of the third grade textbooks?
10. What was in the lavatory, and hungry?

SKELETON CREW
"The Monkey"

Quiz 46

The following questions are from the short story "The Monkey" from the collection *Skeleton Crew*.

1. Which of Hal Shelburn's sons found the monkey?
2. What was the name of Shelburn's other son?
3. What was the name of Shelburn's wife?
4. What company had Shelburn worked for before moving to Texas?
5. What company did Shelburn work for in Texas, and how did his salary stack up to his previous salary?
6. Who was Hal Shelburn's best friend as a child?
7. Who shot Beulah McCaffery?
8. Who brought the news of his mother's death to Shelburn?
9. Where did Shelburn "bury" the toy monkey?
10. Who wrote the article entitled "Mystery of the Dead Fish"?

Quiz 47

The following questions are from the short story "Cain Rose Up" from the collection *Skeleton Crew*.

1. What was Garrish's first name?
2. What was Harry's nickname?
3. Who did the dorm housemother look like?
4. What did Harry's button say?
5. What was the name of the asinine floor-counselor?
6. What was the name of the student who the floor-counselor had sent to the Dean of Men for a drinking offense?
7. Who said pistols and braces were impotency symbols?
8. What kind of rifle did Garrish have in his closet?
9. What was known on campus as the dog kennels?
10. Who was the first person Garrish shot from his dorm window?

"Mrs. Todd's Shortcut"

Quiz 48

The following questions are from the short story "Mrs. Todd's Shortcut" from the collection *Skeleton Crew*.

1. What was the name of the Todds's caretaker?
2. Where did the Todds have their summer home?
3. What was the name of Worth Todd's first wife?
4. What was the name of the guy who got killed by his own dog?
5. What kind of car did Todd's first wife drive?
6. What was the name of the caretaker's brother?
7. When Mrs. Todd drove the caretaker to Bangor, what was the name of the road where he lost his cap to the trees?
8. What was the name of the market where Dave sat and heard the story of Mrs. Todd's shortcut?
9. Where did the caretaker tell people he was moving to when he left Castle Rock?
10. Where did the caretaker actually go?

SKELETON CREW
"The Jaunt"

Quiz 49

The following questions are from the short story "The Jaunt" from the collection *Skeleton Crew*.

1. Where were the Oates headed via the jaunt?
2. What company did Mark Oates work for?
3. How old was Ricky Oates?
4. Who invented the jaunting process?
5. How long did it take to jaunt?
6. What was the name of the book written by C. K. Summers?
7. Who was Rudy Foggia?
8. What did Rudy Foggia say when he emerged from his jaunt?
9. What was the Nil button?
10. What did Ricky Oates say when he emerged from his wide-awake jaunt?

Quiz 50

The following questions are from the short story "The Wedding Gig" from the collection *Skeleton Crew*.

1. What was the name of the small-time racketeer from Shytown?
2. Who owned the speakeasy where the band was playing?
3. How much was the racketeer willing to pay for "the wedding gig"?
4. What was the name of the hall where the wedding gig took place, and where was it located?
5. What was the name of the band's piano player?
6. What were the names of the happy couple?
7. What was the name of the woman in charge of the reception?
8. What was the name of the man the Greek sent to the reception with the "your sister is one fat pig" message?
9. How did the hood's sister kill the Greek?
10. What year did the hood's sister die, what was the cause, and what did she weigh at the time of death?

SKELETON CREW
"The Raft"

The following questions are from the short story "The Raft" from the collection *Skeleton Crew*.

1. Where was the raft?
2. What was the name of the university the four kids attended, and where was it located?
3. What kind of car did Deke own?
4. Who rode in the shotgun seat on the way to the lake?
5. What was the name of Deke's girlfriend?
6. What was the name of Randy's girlfriend?
7. Who was the first student to be eaten by the thing in the water?
8. Which student got sucked through the boards of the raft?
9. Which student got pulled under by her hair?
10. Who was Bon Scott?

Quiz 52

The following questions are from the short story "Word Processor of the Gods" from the collection *Skeleton Crew*.

1. Who built the word processor of the gods?
2. What was the name of Richard Hagstrom's son?
3. Who had once asked Richard Hagstrom "What's a nice guy like you doing with a family like that?"
4. What was the name of the neighbor who helped Hagstrom lug the word processor into the house?
5. What was the name of Richard Hagstrom's drunkard brother?
6. What kind of guitar did Richard's son play?
7. What was the first thing Richard deleted with the word processor?
8. Where did Lina play bingo?
9. What was the name of the priest who had to have his gall-bladder out?
10. What was the last command Richard gave the word processor before it blew up?

SKELETON CREW
"The Man Who Would Not Shake Hands"

The following questions are from the short story "The Man Who Would Not Shake Hands" from the collection *Skeleton Crew*.

1. What was the name of the club's butler?
2. What was the club's address?
3. What was the name of the man who told the story of the man who would not shake hands?
4. How old was the storyteller?
5. Where did the storyteller live and how long had he been living there?
6. What was the name of the man who would not shake hands?
7. Whose father owned three of the largest shoe factories in New England?
8. What member of the club died by innocently grabbing the hand of the man who would not shake hands?
9. Where was the curse put on the man who would not shake hands?
10. How did the man who would not shake hands die?

SKELETON CREW
"Beachworld"

Quiz 54

The following questions are from the short story "Beach-world" from the collection *Skeleton Crew*.

1. What was the registry number of the ship that "fell out of the sky and crashed"?
2. What was the name of the crew member who was killed during the crash?
3. What was the name of the crew member who bottled up all the ship's water?
4. What was the number of Rand's water storage flask?
5. What musical group's tapes did Rand have in his cabin?
6. What kind of rescue ship landed on the planet?
7. What was the name of the rescue ship's captain's assistant who followed the three androids down the gangplank?
8. What was the name of the rescue ship's pilot?
9. Who shot the tranquilizer dart at Rand?
10. How long had the captain been built into treads?

SKELETON CREW
"The Reaper's Image"

Quiz 55

The following questions are from the short story "The Reaper's Image" from the collection *Skeleton Crew*.

1. What was the name of the haunted mirror?
2. Where was the mirror kept?
3. Who was the "keeper" of the mirror?
4. When was the mirror moved, and how much was it insured for?
5. What was the name of the man who was studying the mirror?
6. How did Miss Sandra Bates once try to break the mirror?
7. Who was the 1709 "victim" of the mirror?
8. Who was the 1746 "victim" of the mirror?
9. What was the complete name of the man who made the mirror, and in what period did he live?
10. What did people claim they saw in the mirror?

Quiz 56

The following questions are from the short story "Nona" from the collection *Skeleton Crew*.

1. What was the question Nona asked?
2. What was the name of the diner where the student met Nona?
3. What was the look that people unfailingly gave to guys with long hair?
4. What was the name of the guy who picked up Nona and the narrator after the fight at the diner?
5. What was the phony name Nona used?
6. What was the name of the family who raised the narrator?
7. What was the name of the guy who was dating Betsy Malenfant?
8. What was the name of Nona's fictitious uncle from Castle Rock?
9. Which of the narrator's "brothers" ran away from home?
10. What was the name of the narrator's real brother, and how did he die?

SKELETON CREW
"Survivor Type"

The following questions are from the short story "Survivor Type" from the collection *Skeleton Crew*.

1. On what date did Richard Pine wash up on the island?
2. What were the dimensions of the island?
3. What was Pine's real name?
4. Who was Pine's mother out hustling the day after his father was buried?
5. How much heroin did Pine have when he washed up on the island and what was it worth?
6. What was the name of the "big Chink" who sold Pine the heroin?
7. Who was Ronnie the Enforcer?
8. What was the first body part Pine cut off and ate?
9. What did Pine eat on February 23rd? (Or at least he thought it was February 23rd.)
10. As the story ends, what is Pine eating?

SKELETON CREW
"Uncle Otto's Truck"

The following questions are from the short story "Uncle Otto's Truck" from the collection *Skeleton Crew*.

1. What year was Uncle Otto born?
2. Where did Otto's parents settle when they came to America?
3. What was the name of Uncle Otto's partner in the land deal?
4. Who hooked the wrecker up to the Cresswell after Uncle Otto ditched it?
5. Where was Steve's Pizzaville and what was it before it became a pizza place?
6. Where did Uncle Otto's money go after his death?
7. Who found Uncle Otto's body?
8. When Uncle Otto's body was found, what was pouring out of his mouth and nose?
9. What was the name of the Castle Rock undertaker?
10. What fell out of Uncle Otto's mouth and ended up in his nephew's study?

"Morning Deliveries (Milkman #1)"

Quiz 59

The following questions are from the short story "Morning Deliveries (Milkman #1)" from the collection *Skeleton Crew*.

1. What was the name of the family who had a birdbath?
2. What was the name of the dairy that made the "morning deliveries"?
3. What was the name of the milkman?
4. What was the name of the milkman's friend who worked at the laundry?
5. What did the milkman leave at the McCarthy residence?
6. What did the milkman leave at the Webber residence?
7. What did the milkman leave Miss Ordway?
8. Who was left an empty milk bottle filled with cyanide gas?
9. What did the milkman leave the Walkers?
10. What was matted into a hole in the wall in the empty Merton house?

"Big Wheels: A Tale of the Laundry Game (Milkman #2)"

Quiz 60

The following questions are from the short story "Big Wheels: A Tale of the Laundry Game (Milkman #2)" from the collection *Skeleton Crew*.

1. What kind of car did Rocky drive?
2. What was the name of Rocky's "partner"?
3. What was the name of the laundry where the two guys worked?
4. How long did Rocky serve in 1970 for carrying a concealed weapon?
5. Who was the father of Rocky's wife's baby?
6. How much alimony did Rocky pay his ex-wife?
7. What was the name of the proprietor of Bob's Gas & Service?
8. What was the proprietor's nickname?
9. What were the big washers called?
10. What gave The Devon Woods capital-letter status?

Quiz 61

The following questions are from the short story "Gramma" from the collection *Skeleton Crew*.

1. What was the name of George's mother?
2. What was the name of George's brother?
3. What was the name of George's brother's doctor and what was his phone number?
4. What were the two tortures George's brother repeatedly inflicted upon George?
5. What was the name of the girl George liked?
6. What was the name of the baseball team George played on?
7. What soap opera fan monopolized the area telephone party line from one to six every afternoon?
8. Which of George's uncles died in 1949 of a burst appendix?
9. Where did George's brother go sledding?
10. When Gramma came back from the dead, what did Aunt Flo tell George to do?

"The Ballad of the Flexible Bullet"

Quiz 62

The following questions are from the short story "The Ballad of the Flexible Bullet" from the collection *Skeleton Crew*.

1. Who coined the phrase "flexible bullet"?
2. What was the name of the short story written by Reg Thorpe?
3. What was the name of the novel written by Reg Thorpe?
4. What was the name of the editor who worked for *Logan's* magazine?
5. How did Thorpe sign his response to the editor's offer for the story?
6. What were Fornits?
7. What was Fornus?
8. What was the name of Thorpe's Fornit?
9. Who was the fiction editor for *American Crossings?*
10. Who tried to kill Thorpe's Fornit with a toy ray gun?

SKELETON CREW
"The Reach"

The following questions are from the short story "The Reach" from the collection *Skeleton Crew*.

1. What month, day, and year was Stella Flanders born?
2. Where had Stella Flanders lived her entire life?
3. Where did Larry McKeen work?
4. What's a Reach?
5. What was the name of the island's minister?
6. Who did Stella see smoking a Herbert Tareyton at Russell Bowie's memorial service?
7. What year did Dorrit's Tavern burn down?
8. Who once drove a snowplow through three power poles, knocking out electricity to the town of Raccoon Head for five days?
9. When Stella was found frozen to death on the mainland, what was she wearing on her head?
10. Do the dead sing? Do they love?

V

THE SHORTER
UNCOLLECTED WORKS

"THE FIFTH QUARTER"

Quiz 64

The following questions are from the pseudonymous "John Swithen" short story "The Fifth Quarter." (Even though this story originally appeared in *Cavalier* magazine in April of 1972, it was reprinted [as by Stephen King] in *Twilight Zone* magazine in February 1986, and copies of that issue are still available from many dealers. I think the *TZ* appearance would be the easiest [and least expensive] copy to get your hands on. Try the Overlook Connection.)

1. Keenan's house was an "architectural . . ." what?
2. What was the name of the narrator's partner who had been shot in the stomach and left to die in a boat?
3. What did the narrator feel should have been his partner's epitaph?
4. What was the name of the island where the money was buried?
5. How much money was buried there?
6. Who buried the money and made the map?
7. Whose idea was it to bury the loot?
8. What was the name of Keenan's partner?
9. What kind of television did the Sarge own?
10. Where was Sarge's piece of the map hidden?

"SUFFER THE LITTLE CHILDREN"

Quiz 65

The following questions are from the short story "Suffer the Little Children." (See the Bibliography for details as to where this story is available.)

1. What was Miss Sidley's "game"?
2. What was Miss Sidley's first name?
3. What word did Miss Sidley ask Edward to use in a sentence?
4. Who told Miss Sidley that "Tomorrow a bad thing will happen"?
5. What was the name of the principal?
6. Who gave Miss Sidley smelling salts after she fainted?
7. What was the name of Miss Sidley's brother?
8. Where did Miss Sidley take the children to die?
9. What was the name of the school where Miss Sidley taught?
10. What was the name of Miss Sidley's psychiatrist?

Quiz 66

The following questions are from the short story "The Cat from Hell." (See the Bibliography for details as to where this story is available.)

1. What was the name of the hit man?
2. What was the hit man's "body count"?
3. What was the name of the old man who hired the hit man to kill his cat?
4. Who referred the old man to the hit man?
5. What was the cornerstone of Drogan Pharmaceutical's financial success?
6. What was the name of the old man's sister?
7. What was the name of this sister's lifelong friend?
8. What was the name of the family's hired man?
9. What kind of car did the hit man drive?
10. How did Sam the cat kill the hit man?

"THE NIGHT OF THE TIGER"

Quiz 67

The following questions are from the short story "The Night of the Tiger." (See the Bibliography for details as to where this story is available.)

1. What was the name of the man who visited the circus and just stood watching the tigers?
2. What was the name of the tiger the visitor always kept his eyes on?
3. What was the name of the circus lion-tamer?
4. What was the name of the circus roustabout who was born in Sauk City?
5. What was the name of the circus he was traveling with?
6. What was the name of the red-haired wire walker?
7. What was the name of the bareback rider?
8. How was the circus's cat show billed?
9. What were the names of the other two circus roustabouts?
10. What was the name of the circus's docile black panther?

Quiz 68

The following questions are from the short story "Crouch End." (See the Bibliography for details as to where this story is available.)

1. What were the names of the Crouch End officers who heard the American woman's story about her missing husband?
2. On what lane was the Crouch End police station located?
3. What was the name of the missing American?
4. What were the names of the American woman's kids?
5. What was the name of the sergeant who liked to break pickpockets' fingers?
6. What was the name of the missing American's lawyer colleague who lived in London?
7. In what section of London did this lawyer live?
8. On what building did the American woman see the sign that read "Cthulu Kryon"?
9. Where did Frank Hobbs work?
10. What was the date the American woman told her story to the Crouch End officers?

"BEFORE THE PLAY"

Quiz 69

The following questions are from the five-part prologue to *The Shining* "Before the Play." (See the Bibliography for details as to where this piece is available.)

1. Who bought the Overlook from Bob T. Watson?
2. What was the name of Bob T.'s son who was killed in a riding accident on the grounds of the Overlook?
3. What was the name of the woman who felt a hand grab her wrist from beneath her bed?
4. What was the name of her husband?
5. Who wore a dog costume to the Grand Masquerade?
6. How much did Horace Derwent weigh?
7. How did Jacky Torrance break his arm?
8. What was the name of the West Coast hood that the Gray Old Men saw as "some sort of homicidal stinging insect to be crushed"?
9. Who loaned two guards to the Organization man staying at the Overlook?
10. What was the Overlook at home with?

"Dolan's Cadillac"

Quiz 70

The following questions are from the *Castle Rock* version of the short story "Dolan's Cadillac." (See the Bibliography for details as to where else this story is available.)

1. What was the name of Robinson's wife?
2. What was the name of the health club Robinson joined?
3. What was the name of Robinson's foreman on the Las Vegas Streets and Highways Department?
4. Who taught Robinson how to run the front-end loader?
5. What was the name of the cleaning service that cleaned Dolan's house?
6. In Robinson's nonexistent science fiction short story, how fast was the alien scout vehicle traveling?
7. What were the dimensions of Dolan's grave?
8. How much did a Case-Jordan bucket-loader cost?
9. What kind of car did Robinson's wife drive?
10. What kind of damage did Robinson do to his back digging Dolan's grave?

VI

THE BACHMAN BOOKS

RAGE

Quiz 71

Rage tells the story of a violent and brutal classroom encounter session initiated by one Charles Everett Decker, madman, murderer, and friend. The hours spent in the classroom under Decker's gun changed some students forever, and also destroyed some students irrevocably. *Rage* is another of the remarkably accomplished "early" Stephen King novels that were later released as Bachman novels.

The following questions are from the Richard Bachman novel *Rage*.

1. What's the name of the school where Decker went nuts?
2. What was the name of the algebra teacher who was shot by Decker?
3. What was the name of the school principal?
4. What was the name of the teacher Decker attacked with a pipe wrench?
5. What was the name of the school shrink?
6. On the day Decker "got it on," what classmate was absent due to measles?
7. What was the name of the police officer who shot Decker three times?
8. What was the name of the arrogant student who became the focus of the class's hatred, and who ended up an empty shell sitting on the floor with ink in his hair?
9. What was the name of the judge who committed Decker?
10. After it was all over, what did Decker's mother send him in the asylum?

THE LONG WALK

The Long Walk, written when King was a freshman in college, was rejected by Random House and soon after buried away until it surfaced in 1979 as a Richard Bachman novel. It is a gripping tale of a too-near and too-real future that almost seems possible. *The Long Walk* is an amazing piece of work for a man not two decades old.

The following questions are from the Richard Bachman novel *The Long Walk*.

1. Who won the Long Walk?
2. Who was in charge of the Long Walk and never took off his reflector sunglasses?
3. How many warnings was a Walker allowed before being shot?
4. What was the longest distance a full complement of Walkers had ever covered?
5. What was Ray Garraty's number?
6. Where did the Long Walk begin?
7. What day and time did the Long Walk begin?
8. Who was Sheila?
9. What was the name of Ray Garraty's girlfriend?
10. What was Hint 10?

ROADWORK

Quiz 73

The following questions are from the Richard Bachman novel *Roadwork*.

1. What was the date Bart Dawes visited Harvey's Gun Shop?
2. Who owned Harvey's Gun Shop?
3. What was the name of Dawes's wife?
4. Where did Dawes work?
5. What was the cause of Dawes's son's death?
6. What was the name of the road that ruined twenty years of Dawes's life?
7. What was Dawes's "private drink"?
8. What was the name of the girl Dawes picked up as she was hitchhiking to Las Vegas?
9. What street did Dawes live on and refuse to leave?
10. What was the name of the feature about Dawes that won WHLM a Pulitzer Prize?

Quiz 74

The following questions are from the Richard Bachman novel *The Running Man.*

1. What was the name of Ben Richards' wife?
2. What was the name of the Richards' daughter?
3. Where did the Richards live?
4. What was the government-controlled entertainment system called?
5. What brand of cigarettes did Ben Richards smoke?
6. What was the name of the host of *The Running Man?*
7. What was the name of the game show that had chronic heart, liver, or lung patients walk a treadmill until they either missed a question or had a heart attack?
8. What was the name of the drug that promised "Hallucinogenic Jokes"?
9. Where were the game shows produced?
10. What was the alias Richards bought from Molie Jernigan?

Quiz 75

Thinner tells the story of the ultimate Weight Watchers program: Want to lose those unsightly bulges? You say you're not happy, you want more for your money? Just kill a Gypsy woman, take on a curse, and watch those unwanted pounds just fade away!

The following questions are from the final Richard Bachman novel, *Thinner*.

1. What was the name of the Gypsy woman killed by Billy Halleck?
2. What were the names of Billy Halleck's wife and daughter?
3. Who put the "thinner" curse on Billy Halleck?
4. What was the name of Billy Halleck's law firm?
5. What was the name of the Italian "businessman" who helped Billy get the "thinner" curse removed?
6. What was the name of the restaurant co-owned by the Italian who helped Billy get the curse removed?
7. Where did the Hallecks live?
8. What was Billy's weight the day he was cursed?
9. What was "Ginelli's Pit-Bull Cocktail"?
10. How was the "thinner" curse removed?

VII

THE DARK TOWER BOOKS

THE DARK TOWER : THE GUNSLINGER
"The Gunslinger"

The following questions are from the short story "The Gunslinger" from the collection *The Dark Tower: The Gunslinger*.

1. How many guns did the gunslinger carry?
2. What level of the *khef* had the gunslinger progressed through?
3. Who was the gunslinger tracking?
4. What was the name of the man who lived in the hut in the desert?
5. What was the name of his raven?
6. Who brought the beans to the man in the desert?
7. What was the name of the town the gunslinger had passed through?
8. How did Nort address the gunslinger?
9. What was the name of the bartender at Sheb's?
10. What was the name of the town's woman preacher?

THE DARK TOWER: THE GUNSLINGER
"The Way Station"

The following questions are from the short story "The Way Station" from the collection *The Dark Tower: The Gunslinger*.

1. What was the gunslinger's name?
2. Who had sung the "rain in Spain" rhyme to the gunslinger as a child?
3. What was the name of the boy the gunslinger met at the way station?
4. How did the gunslinger hypnotize the boy in order to get him to tell the story of how he came to be at the way station?
5. In the other world, what was the name of the boy's mother's cook?
6. How did the boy die in the other world?
7. Who spoke to the gunslinger in the basement of the way station?
8. What did the gunslinger find in the basement wall?
9. What was the name of the gunslinger's childhood friend who owned the hawk David?
10. What was the name of the gunslinger's childhood teacher?

THE DARK TOWER: THE GUNSLINGER
"The Oracle and the Mountains"

Quiz 78

The following questions are from the short story "The Oracle and the Mountains" from the collection *The Dark Tower: The Gunslinger*.

1. What was the name of the gunslinger's beloved?
2. How was she killed?
3. What did the gunslinger use to ward off the demon in the stone altar?
4. What drug did the gunslinger take after he and Jake were attacked by the ancient demon in the stone altar?
5. What was the name of the demon who the oracle said had infested the first of "the three"?
6. What was the gunslinger's "gateway to the man in black"?
7. What was the name of the place the gunslinger came from?
8. What was the name of the walled city's cook?
9. How did the man in black appear to the gunslinger in the mountains?
10. How many times did the gunslinger fire at the man in black?

THE DARK TOWER: THE GUNSLINGER
"The Slow Mutants"

Quiz 79

The following questions are from the short story "The Slow Mutants" from the collection *The Dark Tower: The Gunslinger*.

1. What was another name for the Great Hall?
2. What was the name of the enchanter who danced with the gunslinger's mother at the Ball?
3. What did the gunslinger and the boy find set in the ground inside the mountains?
4. What was the gunslinger's weapon in his confrontation with Cort?
5. After besting Cort, what was the teacher's one word of counsel to the victorious gunslinger?
6. How did the Slow Mutants block the handcar?
7. What did the sign say that was written in an ancient root of the High Speech and that hung in the giant hangar inside the mountain?
8. What weapon did the gunslinger take from a weapons shop in the hangar?
9. What were the boy's last words?
10. How many shots did the gunslinger fire at the man in black after the boy's death?

THE DARK TOWER: THE GUNSLINGER
"The Gunslinger and the Dark Man"

Quiz 80

The following questions are from the short story "The Gunslinger and the Dark Man" from the collection *The Dark Tower: The Gunslinger.*

1. What did the man in black give to the gunslinger to cook?
2. What did the gunslinger eat instead, and why?
3. What were the seven tarot cards the man in black turned over when reading the gunslinger's fortune?
4. What was the vision that the man in black sent to the gunslinger as he slept?
5. What was the name of the desert the gunslinger crossed to find the man in black?
6. Who was the man in black's master?
7. Who was greater than the man in black's master?
8. What was the man in black's name?
9. After the man in black said "Let there be light," how long did the gunslinger sleep?
10. What was the "nexus of Time, the nexus of Size"?

THE DARK TOWER II:
THE DRAWING OF THE THREE

Quiz 81

The following questions are from the second volume of the *Dark Tower* series, *The Dark Tower II: The Drawing of the Three.*

1. What creatures attacked Roland and made a noise that sounded like "Did-a-chick"?
2. What was the name of the "prisoner" who tried to smuggle two pounds of cocaine through New York Customs?
3. What was the name of the prisoner's junkie big brother?
4. What enormously popular novel by William Peter Blatty, set in the posh Washington D.C. suburb of Georgetown, concerned the demonic possession of a young girl?
5. What were the names of the two individual personalities that initially made up the schizophrenic Lady of Shadows?
6. What was the name of the Lady of Shadows' chauffeur?
7. What was the name of the Pusher?
8. What was the name of the gun dealer who "sold" Roland four boxes of shells?
9. What was the name of the third person born from the Lady of Shadows?
10. What are the titles of the third and fourth volumes of the *Dark Tower* series?

THE DARK TOWER II:
THE DRAWING OF THE THREE

VIII

THE CREEPSHOW QUIZZES

CREEPSHOW
"Father's Day"

The following questions are from the short story "Father's Day" from the comics collection *Creepshow*.

1. What was the name of the family who met for dinner every Father's Day?
2. What was the name of the aunt who had a summer place in Rome and a lifetime Eurail pass?
3. Who was married to Henry?
4. Who was the patriarch of the clan?
5. What "crime" was this patriarch alleged to have committed?
6. Who was Peter Richard Yarbro?
7. What happened to Yarbro?
8. What was the name of the *real* patriarch of this clan?
9. What was the name of this family's cook?
10. What was the name of Henry's brother-in-law?

"The Lonesome Death of Jordy Verrill"

Quiz 83

The following questions are from the short story "The Lonesome Death of Jordy Verrill" from the comics collection *Creepshow*. (The last two questions are special bonus "For Stephen King Experts Only" questions. They are based on the original *Cavalier* magazine version of this story called "Weeds." If you can't get your hands on this story, then cheat and look at the answers, and then amaze your friends with your King expertise!)

1. Where did Jordy fantasize about bringing his meteor?
2. In his fantasy, what was he offered for the meteor?
3. How much did Jordy actually want?
4. What was the name of Jordy's banker?
5. What was the name of the evangelist Jordy watched on TV?
6. What was the name of his church?
7. What was the name of Jordy's doctor?
8. Who was on call for Jordy's doctor?

"Weeds" Questions:

9. How many types of thinking could Jordy do, and what were they?
10. Jordy wore glasses when he read. What did he usually like to read?

CREEPSHOW
"The Crate"

Quiz 84

The following questions are from the short story "The Crate" from the comics collection *Creepshow*. (The last three questions are special bonus "For Stephen King Experts Only" questions. They are based on the original *Gallery* magazine version of this story called "The Crate." Once again, if you can't get your hands on this story, then cheat and look at the answers, and really amaze your friends with your King knowledge!)

1. What was the name of the university where the crate was found?
2. In what university building was the crate found?
3. Where in this building was the crate found?
4. What did the janitor drop that led to the crate's discovery?
5. What was the name of the janitor?
6. What was the name of the professor who watched the janitor get eaten by the thing in the crate?
7. What was the name of the drunken faculty wife who kept her husband constantly browbeaten and humiliated?

"The Crate" Questions:

8. Who beat out Henry for the English Department chair?
9. Who once found the antique gerbil run at the university?
10. What kind of lighter did Henry use?

125

CREEPSHOW
"Something to Tide You Over"

The following questions are from the short story "Something to Tide You Over" from the comics collection *Creepshow*.

1. Who was having an affair with Becky?
2. What was the name of Becky's husband?
3. What did the husband do to Becky?
4. What did the husband do to her lover?
5. How did the husband show the lover what he'd done to Becky?
6. After the lover died, what did the husband find missing from the beach?
7. What movie had the husband seen a thousand times?
8. After his shower, who came to visit the husband?
9. What did Becky and her lover do to her husband?
10. What was the last thing the husband would ever see?

CREEPSHOW
"They're Creeping Up On You"

The following questions are from the short story "They're Creeping Up On You" from the comics collection *Creepshow*.

1. What was the name of the rich clean freak?
2. What was this guy's motto?
3. Who was his building's superintendent?
4. What was the name of the employee who shot himself?
5. Who called the rich guy with the news of the suicide?
6. What was the name of the employee who took his wife and kids to Disneyworld?
7. What were the names of the exterminators who were supposed to show up by 11:30?
8. Where did the rich guy grow up?
9. What was the name of the cop who took the rich guy's complaint?
10. How did the rich guy die?

IX

THE LATER SHORT STORIES

"The Doctor's Case"

Quiz 87

The following questions are from the short story "The Doctor's Case" from the collection *The New Adventures of Sherlock Holmes*.

1. What was the name of the inspector who worked with Holmes on the case of Lord Hull?
2. What was Sherlock Holmes's address?
3. What was the name of Sherlock Holmes's house-keeper?
4. Where was Lord Hull's house located?
5. What was the name of Lord Hull's solicitor?
6. What was the name of Lord Hull's valet?
7. What were the names of Lord Hull's sons?
8. What was the name of Lord Hull's wife?
9. What was Lord Hull's worth at the time of his death?
10. Who killed Lord Hull?

"Popsy"

Quiz 88

The following questions are from the short story "Popsy" from J. N. Williamson's anthology *Masques II*.

1. Who stole kids for the Turk?
2. What was the name of the mall where the kidnapper found the little boy?
3. What was the Turk's "name"?
4. What was on the T-shirt the kid was wearing?
5. How much did the kidnapper owe Mr. Reggie?
6. Who was the kid looking for?
7. What was the name of the restaurant where the kidnapper claimed he saw the guy that the kid was looking for?
8. How long would the kidnapper get if he got caught snatching the kid?
9. What kind of cologne did Mr. Reggie wear?
10. How did the kidnapper die?

"THE REPLOIDS"

Quiz 89

The following questions are from the short story "The Reploids" from Doug Winter's Dark Harvest collection *Night Visions 5*.

1. What was the date the Reploids became news?
2. What was the name of the Johnny Carson Reploid?
3. What was the name of the Reploid's lawyer?
4. What were the names of the detectives who investigated the assumed kidnapping of Johnny Carson?
5. What was Rule One for the special security functions branch of "Tinsel-Town law enforcement"?
6. According to the Carson Reploid, what was Joan Rivers's real name?
7. What was the name of the lieutenant who watched Cheyney's interrogation of the Reploid from behind a one-way mirror?
8. What color are real NBC Performer's Passes?
9. What color was the Reploid's?
10. Who was on the Reploid's dollar bill?

Quiz 90

The following questions are from the short story "Sneakers" from Doug Winter's Dark Harvest collection *Night Visions 5*.

1. What was the name of the studio that was located in the building that used to be called Music City?
2. Where did John Tell first see the sneakers?
3. What was the name of the guy who hired John Tell?
4. What was the name of the group whose album they were mixing?
5. What was the title of the group's single that entered the *Billboard* chart at number seventy-nine with a bullet?
6. What kind of cigarettes did the third-floor receptionist smoke?
7. What was the name of the group John played bass for in high school?
8. What was the name of the bar where Paul made a gay pass at John?
9. How was Sneakers killed?
10. What was the name of the deli-restaurant on 6th Avenue?

"DEDICATION"

Quiz 91

The following questions are from the short story "Dedication" from the Dark Harvest collection *Night Visions 5*.

1. What was the name of the hotel where Martha Rosewall worked?
2. What was the name of her son?
3. What was the name of the friend Martha told her story to?
4. What was the name of Martha's son's novel?
5. What was the name of Delores's husband?
6. What was the name of the *bruja* woman?
7. Who was the "natural" father of Martha's son?
8. When was *Blaze of Heaven* published?
9. What was the name of Martha's oldest brother who died in a car accident in Biloxi?
10. What was the title of Martha's son's "natural" father's biggest selling book?

Quiz 92

The following questions are from the short story "The Night Flier" from Doug Winter's anthology *Prime Evil*. (See the Bibliography.)

1. What was the name of the periodical that Richard Dees wrote for?
2. What was the name of Dees's editor?
3. What was the name of the "delectable if inept" editor Dees had had an affair with?
4. What was the number of the Night Flier's plane?
5. What periodical and what writer were favored by the audience for *All Shit Grim and Gory?*
6. Who covered the story of the country singer with AIDS?
7. What was the name of the mechanic at the Cumberland County Airport who found a pile of dirt squirming with worms and maggots under the Night Flier's plane?
8. What was the name the Night Flier used?
9. Who did Dees consider the only truly honest man he'd ever met?
10. What book was found on the dead body of Ellen Sarch?

Quiz 93

The following questions are from the uncollected short story "My Pretty Pony."

This story is a touching and tender story of the relationship between a grandfather and his grandson. Stan Wiater told me this story reminded him of Ernest Hemingway and Ray Bradbury, and I'd have to agree.

Since the moment I read it, I have never forgotten the passage where King describes the grandfather's death: ". . . Grandpa's pony had kicked down Grandpa's fences and gone over all the hills of the world. Wicked heart, wicked heart. Pretty, but with a wicked heart."

Once again (as with "The Last Rung on the Ladder" and "The Body"), King proves to his critics that he is not just a superb horror writer, he is a superb *writer*.

Period. Case closed.

(See the Bibliography for details on the limited and the mass market editions of this story.)

1. What was Grandpa's name?
2. What was the name of his grandson?
3. What was the town, state, and locale where the grandson took instruction in 1962?
4. What was Gramma's motto?
5. Who cheated at hide and seek?
6. Grandpa gave his grandson something that was once stepped on in a beerjoint in Utica. What was it?
7. What was "my pretty pony"?
8. Who used to own "the mercantile"?
9. What was the name of the local clergyman?
10. What were the words the grandson never forgot—"words almost thrown away, lost in the wind"?

"RAINY SEASON"

Quiz 94

The following questions are from the short story "Rainy Season." (See the Bibliography for details as to where this story is available.)

1. What was the name of the town where the rainy season took place?
2. What was the name of the young couple on sabbatical for the summer?
3. What school was picking up the tab for their summer?
4. Where did the couple plan on staying for the summer?
5. What was the name of the old man on the front porch of the Mercantile?
6. What was the name of the old man's lady friend?
7. How often did the rainy season come around, and on what date did it take place?
8. What specifically happened during the rainy season?
9. What was the name of Milly Cousins's great aunt?
10. How did the couple on sabbatical die?

"HOME DELIVERY"

Quiz 95

The following questions are from the short story "Home Delivery" from the anthology *Book of the Dead*. (See the Bibliography.)

1. What was the name of Maddie Pace's husband?
2. What was Maddie's old name?
3. What was the name of Maddie's clergyman?
4. Where did Maddie and her mother live after George Sullivan died?
5. What was the name of the living satellite discovered by the British astronomer Humphrey Dagbolt?
6. What was the title of the *Inside View* article that referred to the film *The Night of the Living Dead*?
7. Who was the only Jew on the island?
8. How could the zombies be stopped?
9. What was the name of the man who insisted that his friends blow him to smithereens, rather than allow him to come back to life as a zombie?
10. What was the name of the island family that owned a satellite dish?

X

MISCELLANEOUS QUIZZES

"ALL SHOOK UP!"
A Mixed-Up Muddle

Quiz 96

Rearrange the following jumbles into the titles of some of Stephen King's novels and short stories. Most of the titles are of King's most popular works, but there are few in there that are a bit obscure. Once again, try Doug Winter's *Stephen King: The Art of Darkness* for complete bibliographic information . . . and Dogo Culk!

1. TOLL SESAM
2. RATEAR SHET VINDS
3. LETAB NURDGOT
4. SHRINT ICE
5. FLARK HETHAD
6. AKASEH WO HOD HULNWOT HEN STAMND
7. ERRACI
8. LEP THANT
9. THTM CREE OYNK SKOM
10. HINT REN
11. IR RAT FESTER
12. SWHODEER HAANK MATNIOP DARTH WITHY NARS
13. NODEZA DEHTE
14. NNIIHHSTEG
15. TEPHALY FEBORE

"NASTY GIRLS"

The following multiple-choice questions all concern themselves with Stephen King's female characters.

1. Which of the following girls threw sanitary napkins at Carrie White?
   a. Annie Wilkes
   b. Chris Hargensen
   c. Stella Randolph
2. The "lover's triangle" in *Christine* consisted of Arnie Cunningham, Christine, and . . .
   a. Leigh Cabot
   b. Wendy Torrance
   c. Ophelia Todd
3. Which of the following women created the Great Hospital?
   a. Alice
   b. Queen Sasha
   c. Cathy Scott
4. Gage Creed's sister was named . . .
   a. Georgette
   b. Carrie
   c. Ellie
5. Brett Camber's mother's name was . . .
   a. Charity
   b. Felicity
   c. Harmony
6. The woman in charge of the New England Poetry Caravan was . . .
   a. Odetta Holmes
   b. Patricia McCardle
   c. Regina Cunningham

7. The author of *The Buffalo Soldiers* was . . .
   a. Bobbi Anderson
   b. Tabitha King
   c. Louanne Deserio
8. What was the name of the young girl who wanted to hear the story of the Jaunt?
   a. Lois Perrault
   b. Patty Oates
   c. Hall and Oates
9. Which of the following women was a Loser?
   a. Diana Rucklehouse
   b. Bev Rogan
   c. Lynn
10. Ben Mears's girlfriend was . . .
   a. Mrs. Reppler
   b. Sue Norton
   c. Trixie Norton
11. What was the name of the teacher Charlie Decker shot in the head?
   a. Mrs. Underwood
   b. Miss Bird
   c. Miss Marble
12. What was the name of Chico's girlfriend?
   a. Janet
   b. Janelle
   c. Jane
13. Charlie McGee's mother's name was . . .
   a. Nikki
   b. Ricki
   c. Vicky
14. What was the name of Johnny Smith's mother?
   a. Emily
   b. Vera
   c. Lenore
15. What was the name of the 108-year-old black woman who survived Captain Trips?
   a. Mother Abagail
   b. Mother Teresa
   c. Fran Goldsmith

"The Boys Are Back in Town"

The following multiple-choice questions all concern themselves with Stephen King's male characters.

1. Which of the following men was once a Bible salesman?
   a. Greg Stillson
   b. Joe Parcella
   c. Ray Brower
2. Who told the Shop agents "Show me your warrant or get the Christ off my property"?
   a. Andy McGee
   b. Irv Manders
   c. Joe Badamo
3. Who had to admit to himself that when it rained in Cornwall, it rained harder than anywhere else in England?
   a. Billy Nolan
   b. Dave Hinchberger
   c. Ian Carmichael
4. Which of the following men was NOT a Shawshank guard?
   a. Byron Hadley
   b. Tim Youngblood
   c. Andy Dufresne
5. Who was the phys ed teacher at the Tarker's Mills grammar school?
   a. Herman Coslaw
   b. Arnie Cunningham
   c. Kenny Franklin
6. Who referred Dick Morrison to Quitters, Inc.?
   a. Vic Donatti
   b. Jimmy McCann
   c. Steve Rapuano

7. Who punctured holes in Jack Torrance's tires?
   a. George Hatfield
   b. Bruce Trevor
   c. Brett Camber
8. Who was the Major's son?
   a. Garraty
   b. Stebbins
   c. Scramm
9. Who was the father of Fran Goldsmith's child?
   a. George Stark
   b. Eddie Dean
   c. Jessie Rider
10. Who designed the dam in the Barrens?
    a. Richie Tozier
    b. Bill Denbrough
    c. Ben Hanscom
11. What was the name of the English teacher in the town of Jerusalem's Lot?
    a. Matt Burke
    b. Grover Verrill
    c. Jordy Verrill
12. Who killed Hans Morris?
    a. Springheel Jack
    b. Johnny Renshaw
    c. Charlie Hogan
13. What was the name of the reporter who tracked the Night Flier?
    a. Jud Crandall
    b. Richard Dees
    c. Stu Redman
14. What was the name of Vic Trenton's partner?
    a. Roger Breakstone
    b. Gary Dermer
    c. Ralph White
15. Who suggested in his *Deptford Trilogy* that our attitude toward magic and magicians in large part indicates our attitude toward reality?
    a. Stephen King
    b. John Updike
    c. Robertson Davies

STEPHEN KING'S "SCHOOL DAZE"

Quiz 99

Considering he used to be a teacher, it's not too surprising to find many of Stephen King's stories set in academic environments.

This quiz asks you to match the educational institution in the left column with the novel or story in which it appears from the right column.

_____ 1. New Sharon Teachers' College

_____ 2. Acorn Street Grammar School

_____ 3. Ewen High School

_____ 4. Horlicks University

_____ 5. Harold Davis High School

_____ 6. Libertyville High School

_____ 7. Thayer School

_____ 8. Summer Street School

_____ 9. Cleaves Mills High School

_____10. Placerville High School

A. "Here There Be Tygers"

B. "Suffer the Little Children"

C. *Rage*

D. *The Dead Zone*

E. "The Raft"

F. *Christine*

G. "Sometimes They Come Back"

H. *Carrie*

I. "Strawberry Spring"

J. *The Talisman*

"MATCH THE MONSTERS"

Quiz 100

This quiz asks you to match the "monster" from the left column with the work in the right. In some cases, there is more than one monster from the same work, as well as the opposite: in a few cases, there is more than one correct work for one monster. Try and get them all!

____ 1. A haunted hotel	A. *Rage*
____ 2. Vampires	B. "Battleground"
____ 3. A single, psycho-pathic teenager	C. *It*
____ 4. The Boogeyman	D. "Trucks"
____ 5. A haunted amusement park	E. *The Long Walk*
____ 6. The Mummy	F. "Graveyard Shift"
____ 7. A teenage voodoo expert	G. "I Am the Doorway"
____ 8. A demonic shirt-folding machine	H. *The Shining*
____ 9. A malicious, sadistic millionaire	I. "Night Surf"
____10. Living, vengeful toy soldiers	J. *The Tommyknockers*
____11. Spoiled beer	K. "Gray Matter"
____12. Ghosts	L. "The Mangler"
____13. Modern medicine	M. "Nona"
____14. A killer flu	N. "The Boogeyman"
____15. The government	O. "The Mist"
____16. Zombies	P. "Sometimes They Come Back"
____17. A house that grows by itself	Q. *Pet Sematary*

149

____18. Living, malevolent trucks   R. "The Ledge"

____19. A cat from Hell   S. "I Know What You Need"

____20. A man who steals children   T. "Strawberry Spring"

____21. A haunted toilet stall   U. "Survivor Type"

____22. The Wolfman   V. *'Salem's Lot*

____23. Giant mutant rats   W. "Gramma"

____24. A psychopathic, schizophrenic serial killer   X. "I Was a Teenage Grave Robber"

____25. A Corn God   Y. "Children of the Corn"

____26. A rabid St. Bernard   Z. *Misery*

____27. Unwanted precognitive abilities   AA. *Firestarter*

____28. A mad scientist   BB. *The Eyes of the Dragon*

____29. Unwanted pyrokinetic abilities   CC. *Cujo*

____30. The Wendigo   DD. "The Cat from Hell"

____31. A giant alien spider   EE. "The Woman in the Room"

____32. A beautiful dead ghost   FF. "It Grows On You"

____33. Slow Mutants   GG. "One for the Road"

____34. A dead grandmother   HH. *The Dead Zone*

____35. A Werewolf   II. *The Dark Tower: The Gunslinger*

____36. Evil Twinners   JJ. "Beachworld"

____37. A haunted mirror   KK. "The Glass Floor"

____38. An evil wizard   LL. "Sneakers"

____39. Leeches   MM. "My Pretty Pony"

____40. A Gypsy curse   NN. *The Talisman*

____41. A killer nurse   OO. *Cycle of the Werewolf*

____42. A mist   PP. "The Reaper's Image"

____43. The monster in the water   QQ. *Thinner*

BRANDED!
A Brand Name Quiz

Quiz 101

Fill in the blanks with the correct brand name from the works of Stephen King.

1. When Charlie McGee was a year old, her father had to put _____ on her cheek because she had unwittingly caused her pillow to smolder and burn her as she slept.
2. Margaret White had a _____ cuckoo clock in her living room.
3. When Dennis Guilder got home from school, he had a can of _____ as a snack.
4. As Roger Chatsworth snowshoed with Johnny Smith, Chatsworth offered Johnny a drink of _____.
5. Church Creed ate _____ cat food.
6. After Timothy Breakstone's death, Roger Breakstone became a closet _____ chugger.
7. _____ magazine ran an article on Warden Norton's "Inside-Out" program.
8. On his way home from work, Billy Halleck found two packages of _____ in his glove compartment.
9. Rocky and Leo were both "drunk as the last lords of creation" on _____ beer.
10. After Russell Bowie drowned in the Reach, a nice little going-away party was held for him, complete with _____ punch and little cream-cheese sandwiches.
11. Bill Denbrough used _____ paraffin to waterproof his brother Georgie's paper boat.
12. Kurt Dussander's brand of cigarettes was _____.
13. Andy Torgeson and Claudell Weems were attacked by a flying _____ machine.

152

14. The food supplies left for the Torrances included a whole bag of _____ pies.
15. Dr. McCarron had once heard of a woman who gave herself an abortion with a broken _____ bottle.
16. John helped his mother commit suicide by feeding her _____ capsules.
17. Before Paul's surgery, Annie sterilized his foot with _____ solution.
18. When Norman Bruett's house blew up, _____ toys ended up all over Laurel Street.
19. Gordie Lachance offered his dad one of his _____ candies.
20. On their way home, Wolf, Richard, and Jack stopped at _____, where Wolf ate all twenty-one pieces of a Family-Style Bucket.

"AT THE MOVIES"

Quiz 102

Match the actor or director from the column on the left with the Stephen King movie he or she is associated with from the column on the right.

___ 1.	Sissy Spacek	A.	*CREEPSHOW*
___ 2.	Rob Reiner	B.	*CHRISTINE*
___ 3.	Jack Nicholson	C.	*CHILDREN OF*
___ 4.	Heather Locklear		*THE CORN*
___ 5.	Tobe Hooper	D.	*PET SEMATARY*
___ 6.	Denise Crosby	E.	*THE RUNNING*
___ 7.	Stephen King		*MAN*
___ 8.	Emilio Estevez	F.	*CARRIE*
___ 9.	Candy Clark	G.	*FIRESTARTER*
___10.	Linda Hamilton	H.	*SILVER BULLET*
___11.	Harry Dean	I.	*CAT'S EYE*
	Stanton	J.	*THE DEAD ZONE*
___12.	Dee Wallace	K.	*STAND BY ME*
___13.	Gary Busey	L.	*THE SHINING*
___14.	Christopher	M.	*'SALEM'S LOT*
	Walken	N.	*CUJO*
___15.	Arnold	O.	*MAXIMUM*
	Schwarzenegger		*OVERDRIVE*

"WHO'S WHO?"

Quiz 103

Match the character from the column on the left with the Stephen King work he, she (or it) appeared in from the column on the right.

____ 1.	Bob Gray	A.	"Mrs. Todd's
____ 2.	Bobbi Anderson		Shortcut"
____ 3.	Jud Crandall	B.	*Misery*
____ 4.	John Rainbird	C.	*The Plant*
____ 5.	Charles Decker	D.	*Pet Sematary*
____ 6.	Mark Petrie	E.	"The Monkey"
____ 7.	Mrs. Carmody	F.	"Jerusalem's Lot"
____ 8.	Zoltan	G.	*The Stand*
____ 9.	Marty Coslaw	H.	*Rage*
____10.	Paul Sheldon	I.	*The Talisman*
____11.	Larry Underwood	J.	"The Doctor's Case"
____12.	Ophelia Todd	K.	*The Drawing of the*
____13.	Hal Shelburn		*Three*
____14.	Carlos Detweiller	L.	"The Mist"
____15.	Charles Boone	M.	*Cycle of the Werewolf*
____16.	Barton Dawes	N.	*Firestarter*
____17.	Detta Walker/	O.	*'Salem's Lot*
	Odetta Holmes	P.	*The Tommyknockers*
____18.	Sherlock Holmes	Q.	"Apt Pupil"
____19.	Kurt Dussander	R.	*Roadwork*
____20.	Wolf	S.	*It*
		T.	"The Gunslinger"

"SAY WHAT??"

Quiz 104

Identify the speaker of the following quotations.

1. "You little tin-weasel peckerwood loony's son! I'll see your mother gets an invitation to go down and talk to the judge in court about what you done to my dawg!"

2. "I'm picturing your heart, Momma. It's easier when you see things in your mind. Your heart is a big red muscle. Mine goes faster when I use my power. But yours is going a little slower now. A little slower."

3. "Suppose there is a little girl out there someplace this morning who has within her, lying dormant only for the time being, the power to someday crack the very planet in two like a china plate in a shooting gallery?"

4. "No charge to you, Mr. Torrance. Your money is no good here. Orders from the manager."

5. "At Chernobyl they killed the kids. Don't you understand that? The ones ten years old, the ones *in utero*. Most may still be alive, but they are dying right now while we stand here with our drinks in our hands. Some can't even read yet. Most will never kiss a girl in passion. Right now while we're standing here with our drinks in our hands."

6. "I know a creep when I see one, and I think I'm lookin' at one right now. You're on probation, kid. You screw around with me just one time and it don't matter how much you paid up in front, I'll put you out on your ass."

7. "Nope, nothing wrong here."

156

8. "If they caught them they made sure that they could go on working . . . but they *also* made sure they would never run again. The operation was called *hobbling*, Paul, and that is what I'm going to do to you."
9. Go slow past the Drawers, gunslinger. While you travel with the boy, the man in black travels with your soul in his pocket."
10. "Hi-yo Silver, AWAYYYYYYY!"

"... THE TRUTH INSIDE THE LIE ..."
A True or False Quiz

Quiz 105

Answer true or false to the following statements about Stephen King's tales.

1. Jim Gardener was the first person to find the spaceship in the earth.
2. Jack Torrance was a published writer when he took the job at the Overlook.
3. The name of Vic Trenton's advertising agency was Ads Unlimited, Inc.
4. The name of the drug Annie Wilkes administered to Paul Sheldon was Novril.
5. Bill Denbrough committed suicide rather than once again confront IT.
6. George's Gramma was a witch.
7. The Trashcan Man died from Captain Trips.
8. 'Salem's Lot was in Nebraska.
9. The first living thing to Jaunt was a mouse.
10. After destroying the Shop, Charlie McGee brought her story to the *New York Times*.
11. Jordy Verrill sold his meteor for $200.
12. Johnny killed his mother with an overdose of Darvon Complex.
13. Laura DeLoessian was Lily Cavanaugh Sawyer's Twinner.
14. Dolan drove a Buick.
15. Johnny Smith was injured in an accident involving his VW and a milk truck.
16. Richard Dees wrote for the *National Enquirer*.
17. Thad Beaumont's "George Stark" writing tool of choice was a red flair.
18. Sandra Stansfield had a boy.
19. Ben Richards was a contestant on *Treadmill to Bucks*.
20. The first part of his anatomy that Richard Pine ate was his left foot.

"WHAT A WAY TO GO!"

Quiz 106

Stephen King has killed off his characters in a variety of nefarious ways, and "What a Way to Go!" tests your knowledge of the Killer King.

This quiz requires you to match the means of death from Column 1 with the victim in Column 2, and the work in which the character and demise appeared from Column 3. (There are only nineteen works in Column 3 because one work is cited twice.)

Column 1

_____ 1. Death by telekinetically caused cardiac arrest
_____ 2. Death by self-cannibalization
_____ 3. Suicide by sticking his arm down a garbage disposal
_____ 4. Being buried alive in a Cadillac
_____ 5. Being eaten by a Hadley-Watson Model-6 Speed Ironer and Folder
_____ 6. Being eaten by giant mutant rats
_____ 7. Death by a cat eating his way out of his stomach
_____ 8. Death by skull fracture, complicated by being struck in the back by a hurled Royal typewriter and having flaming manuscript pages shoved down her throat
_____ 9. Death by sand ingestion
_____10. Death by being pulled through a crack in a raft by a floating blob
_____11. Death by being pushed in front of, and subsequently run over by, a blue 1976 Cadillac
_____12. Being deleted by a word processor
_____13. Being eaten by a St. Bernard
_____14. Being run over by a trailer truck
_____15. Being turned into a vampire

_____16. Getting shot while climbing a halftrack
_____17. Getting shot in the stomach, getting his intes-
tines tangled up under a dead man's chin, and
flying a plane into a skyscraper
_____18. Being turned into a giant mutant slug amoeba
by bad beer
_____19. Being eaten by a giant mutant slug amoeba
_____20. Being physically invaded by aliens with lots of
eyes, and then shooting himself with a shotgun

Column 2		*Column 3*	
A.	Halston	AA.	*Misery*
B.	Lina Hagstrom	BB.	*'Salem's Lot*
C.	Gage Creed	CC.	"The Cat from Hell"
D.	Dolan		
E.	Hank Olson	DD.	"I Am the Doorway"
F.	Deke		
G.	Foreman Hall	EE.	"Graveyard Shift"
H.	Danny Glick	FF.	*Firestarter*
I.	Ben Richards	GG.	*Carrie*
J.	Richard Pine	HH.	"The Way Station"
K.	Margaret White	II.	"Gray Matter"
L.	Adelle Frawley	JJ.	*The Running Man*
M.	Richie Grenadine	KK.	"Dolan's Cadillac"
N.	Dr. Herman Pynchot	LL.	"The Mangler"
O.	Arthur	MM.	*Cujo*
P.	Rand	NN.	"Word Processor of the Gods"
Q.	Annie Wilkes		
R.	Gary Pervier	OO.	"Beachworld"
S.	Jake Chambers	PP.	"The Raft"
T.	Two young girls and a Salvation Army wino	QQ.	*Pet Sematary*
		RR.	*The Long Walk*
		SS.	"Survivor Type"

Epilogue

THE STEPHEN KING "SHOW NO MERCY AND TAKE NO PRISONERS" QUIZ

Quiz 107

This quiz is hard.

Real hard.

And one of the reasons it's so hard is that there are absolutely no clues given as to what works the questions were drawn from.

Throughout *The Stephen King Quiz Book*, no matter how difficult a question seemed to be on first reading, there was usually a built-in clue: You almost always began knowing the novel or short story where the answer could be found. With this "No Mercy" quiz, the questions are drawn from the entire canon of King's work, and they concern themselves with either characters, events, or locales that will probably not be immediately recognizable to the average King reader.

Let's see what you're made of, huh?

1. Where are Marie Curie's notebooks?
2. What bank held Lars Ancasters's mortgage?
3. Who owned a light gray 1971 Ford Econoline van with Maine license number 641-644?
4. What does rattlesnake taste like?
5. What tune passed for racy out in the boondocks in 1927?
6. "What do you hear? What does the land command?"
7. Who was a helluva sniffer?
8. Who was always writing about Dimensions?
9. Complete the following verse:
   "Jesus watches from the wall,
   But his face is cold as stone,
   And if he loves me
   As she tells me . . ."
10. What is Stephen King's middle name?

161

THE ANSWERS

Quiz 1

1. Portland, Maine. 2. September 21, 1947; Carrie White. 3. Donald and Nellie Ruth King. 4. King is married to novelist Tabitha Spruce King. 5. Bangor, Maine. 6. His childhood friend Chris Chesley. 7. The pseudonym Stephen King used to release the five "Richard Bachman" novels. 8. *Castle Rock.* 9. "I Was a Teenage Grave Robber." 10. "The Glass Floor." 11. The University of Maine at Orono. 12. Naomi Rachel, Joseph Hillstrom, and Owen Philip. 13. *Carrie*, in 1974. 14. George Romero's *Knightriders* in 1981 (with his wife Tabitha) and *Creepshow* in 1982, King's own *Maximum Overdrive* in 1986, Michael Gornick's *Creepshow 2* in 1987, and Mary Lambert's *Pet Sematary* in 1989. 15. The Boston Red Sox. 16. The novelists Richard Matheson, John D. MacDonald, and Don Robertson. 17. Donald M. Grant, Publisher. 18. Philtrum Press. 19. *Time* magazine. 20. Viking in hardcover, and NAL/Signet in paperback.

Quiz 2

The following answers give the author of the epigraph quote first, then the work from which it was taken (if applicable), and finally the Stephen King work that the epigraph led off.

1. Flaubert; *Different Seasons.* 2. John F. Kennedy; *The Long Walk.* 3. Goya; *The Shining.* 4. Janis Joplin; *Christine* (the chapter "On the Bleachers"). 5. Doris Lessing, *The Golden Notebook; The Tommyknockers* (Book III: "The Tommyknockers."). 6. W.H. Auden, "Musée des Beaux Arts"; *Cujo.* 7. Montaigne; *Misery* (Part II: "Misery"). 8. John's Gospel (paraphrase); *Pet Sematary* (Part I:

"The Pet Sematary"). 9. Bob Dylan; *'Salem's Lot* (Part III: "The Deserted Village"). 10. Norman Whitfield, "I Heard It Through the Grapevine"; *Different Seasons*. 11. Neil Young; *It*. 12. Steely Dan, "Deacon Blues"; *Christine* (the chapter "Football Woes"). 13. Bruce Springsteen, "Jungle Land"; *The Stand*. 14. *The Koran*; "Dolan's Cadillac." 15. Child's rime; *Cycle of the Werewolf*. 16. Mark Twain, *Huckleberry Finn; The Talisman*. 17. Peter Straub, *Ghost Story; Danse Macabre*. 18. Martin Scorsese's *Mean Streets; It* ("Derry: The Second Interlude"). 19. Creedence Clearwater Revival, "It Came Out of the Sky"; *The Tommyknockers* (Book II: "Tales of Heaven"). 20. Art Fleming, "Jeopardy"; *The Long Walk* (Chapter 3).

Quiz 3

1. "Nona," *Skeleton Crew* 2. *The Shining* 3. *The Running Man* 4. "Suffer the Little Children" 4. "Gray Matter," *Night Shift* 6. *The Tommyknockers* 7. "The Ballad of the Flexible Bullet," *Skeleton Crew* 8. *Misery* 9. *Firestarter* 10. "The Lawnmower Man," *Night Shift* 11. "Sneakers," *Night Visions* 5 12. "For Owen" (poem), *Skeleton Crew* 13. "The End of the Whole Mess" 14. *The Stand* 15. *'Salem's Lot* 16. "Trucks," *Night Shift* 17. "Beachworld," *Skeleton Crew* 18. "Uncle Otto's Truck," *Skeleton Crew* 19. *The Eyes of the Dragon* 20. "For the Birds"

Quiz 4

People   1. Margaret White. 2. Ralph White. 3. Rita Desjardin. 4. Henry (Hank) Grayle. 5. Peter (Morty) Morton. 6. Chris Hargensen. 7. Billy Nolan. 8. Sue Snell. 9. Tommy Ross. 10. Carrie White.

Places   1. Ewen High School. 2. Barker Street Grammar School. 3. Blue Ribbon Laundry. 4. North Chamberlain, Maine. 5. 47 Carlin Street, Chamberlain, Maine 02249. 6. 19 Back Chamberlain Road, Chamberlain, Maine 02249. 7. Shuber's Five and Ten. 8. Teddy Duchamp. 9. Royal Knob, Tennessee. 10. A graveyard.

Things   1. Female breasts, according to Margaret White. 2. The closet. 3. June 1–2, 1979. 4. A 1977

Plymouth. 5. The Billy Bosnan Band or Josie and the Moonglows. 6. "500 Miles," "Lemon Tree," or "Mr. Tambourine Man." 7. A bucket of pig's blood. 8. *My Name Is Susan Snell*. 9. Hemorrhage, shock, coronary occlusion, and/or coronary thrombosis (possible). 10. May 27, 1979.

Quiz 5

People   1. Ben Mears. 2. Susan Norton. 3. Larry Crockett. 4. Eva Miller. 5. Corey Bryant. 6. Mark Petrie. 7. Hubie Marsten. 8. Kurt Barlow. 9. Richard Throckett Straker. 10. Matthew Burke.

Places   1. Babs' Beauty Boutique. 2. Marsten's Hill. 3. The Village Washtub. 4. Crockett's Southern Maine Insurance and Realty. 5. Kittery. 6. St. Andrew's. 7. Barlow and Straker's Furniture Shop. 8. Los Zapatos. 9. Railroad Street. 10. Jerusalem's Lot.

Things   1. His first was *Conway's Daughter*, his second, *Air Dance*, and his third, *Billy Said Keep Going*. 2. The *Ledger*. 3. August 12, 1939. 4. A 1939 or 1940 Packard. 5. "Too Far to Jump." 6. A .22 caliber target pistol. 7. Continental Land and Realty. 8. A Video King. 9. *Cosmopolitan*. 10. The Royal River.

Quiz 6

People   1. Wendy. 2. Danny. 3. Tony. 4. Stuart Ullman. 5. Dick Hallorann. 6. Albert Shockley. 7. Delbert Grady. 8. Lloyd. 9. Delores Vickery. 10. George Hatfield.

Places   1. Sidewinder. 2. Stovington, Vermont. 3. Room 217. 4. The Red Arrow Lodge in western Maine. 5. St. Petersburg, Florida. 6. The Jack and Jill Nursery School. 7. In the basement of the Overlook. 8. The Colorado Lounge. 9. Room 300, the Presidential Suite. 10. Arapahoe Street.

Things   1. The shining. 2. A superb roque court and a giant hedge topiary. 3. *The Little School*. 4. REDRUM. 5. 110. 6. "Concerning the Black Holes." 7. Martians 8. A Volkswagen. 9. *Strange Resort, The Story of the Overlook Hotel*. 10. A Spanish Llama .38.

Quiz 7

People   1. Larry Underwood. 2. Nick Andros. 3. Randall Flagg. 4. Harold Lauder. 5. Donald Merwin Elbert. 6. Mother Abagail Freemantle. 7. He was known as Kojak, but his real name was Big Steve. 8. Geraldo. 9. Glen Bateman. 10. Peter Goldsmith-Redman.

Places   1. US 93 just north of Arnette, Texas. 2. Ogunquit, Maine. 3. In Stovington. 4. The Brownsville Minimum Security Station. 5. In Boulder, Colorado. 6. In eastern Nebraska. 7. In Indiana. 8. Woodsville Community College. 9. Las Vegas, Nevada. 10. Las Vegas, Nevada.

Things   1. Captain Trips. 2. The Eye. 3. Project Blue. 4. Veronal. 5. A1641OUSAF. 6. September 5, 1985. 7. The Tattered Remnants. 8. It was called "Speak Your Piece" and it was hosted by Ray Flowers. 9. M-O-O-N. 10. A .357 Magnum.

Quiz 8

People   1. Deputy Sheriff Frank Dodd. 2. Herb and Vera Smith. 3. Sarah Bracknell. 4. Greg Stillson. 5. Ngo Phat. 6. Richard Dees. 7. Dr. Weizak. 8. Greg Stillson's right-hand man. 9. Chuck Chatsworth. 10. Alma Frechette, Pauline Toothaker, Cheryl Moody, Carol Dunbarger, Etta Ringgold, and Mary Kate Hendrasen.

Places   1. Pownal, Maine. 2. South Paris, Maine. 3. RFD #1, Pownal, Maine. 4. The 4th Street Phoenix Sporting Goods Store. 5. Cleaves Mills High School. 6. Cathy's Roadhouse. 7. The Shade. 8. Runaround Pond in Durham, Maine. 9. The Eastern Maine Medical Center Emergency Room. 10. Hart Hall.

Things   1. May 17, 1975. 2. "The whole wad on nineteen," "One way or the other," and "My girl's sick." 3. 55 months. 4. The American Society of the Last Times. 5. The dead zone. 6. *Inside View* magazine. 7. The Laughing Tiger. 8. *Citizen Kane*. 9. He paid $11,000 on an income of $36,000. 10. The Wheel of Fortune.

Quiz 9

People   1. Charlene Roberta McGee. 2. Andy McGee. 3. Vicky Tomlinson McGee. 4. Norma and Irv Manders. 5. Captain (Cap) Hollister. 6. Orville Jamieson. 7. John Rainbird. 8. Dr. Herman Pynchot. 9. Dr. Joseph Wanless. 10. "Frank Burton."

Places   1. Harrison State College in Ohio. 2. Jason Gearneigh Hall. 3. Longmont, Virginia. 4. In Vietnam. 5. The Buckeye Room. 6. The Free Children's Nursery School in Harrison, New York. 7. Notions 'n' Novelties. 8. The Ohio Semi-Conductor Plant. 9. Sanibel Island, Florida. 10. Maui.

Things   1. August 1980. 2. "Axon." 3. "The push"—an ability to "persuade" people to do what he wanted them to do. 4. RFD #5, Baillings Road, Hastings Glen, New York. 5. Charlie's ability to start fires. 6. An experimental chemical compound injected into twelve college students. Dr. Wanless described it as "essentially an hypnotic and mild hallucinogenic." It caused Charlie McGee to be born with the ability to start fires with her mind. 7. The DSI. The Department of Scientific Intelligence. 8. "Brow." 9. *Rolling Stone.* 10. Orville Jamieson's gun. It was a .357 Magnum.

Quiz 10

People   1. Joe Camber. 2. Donna Trenton. 3. Tad Trenton. 4. Roger Breakstone. 5. The Cookie Sharpshooter. 6. Gary Pervier. 7. Steve Kemp. 8. The Sharp Cereal Professor. 9. Mr. Steigmeyer. 10. The alias Steve Kemp used when he called Vic Trenton's office.

Places   1. Castle Rock, Maine. 2. Bridgton, Maine. 3. Connecticut. 4. The Mellow Tiger. 5. Seven Oaks Farm, on Town Road No. 3. 6. Boise, Idaho, and Scranton, Pennsylvania. 7. South Paris. 8. The ficitious company made up by Steve Kemp when he called Vic Trenton's office. 9. Kennebunk Beach. 10. Westport, Connecticut.

Things   1. Ad Worx. 2. February 1945. 3. Gaines Meal and Ralston-Purina. 4. A Pinto. 5. An incantation

Vic made up to keep the monsters out of Tad's room. 6.
A question mark. 7. Tadder. 8. 83 Larch Street, Castle
Rock, Maine. 9. It consisted of 25 percent Bird's Eye
frozen orange juice and 75 percent Popov vodka. 10.
All-Grain Blend, Bran-16, Cocoa Bears, Red Razberry
Zingers, or Twinkles.

Quiz 11

People   1. Christine, a red 1958 Plymouth Fury. 2.
Buddy Repperton. 3. Leigh Cabot. 4. Dennis Guilder.
5. Rudy Junkins. 6. Roland LeBay. 7. Barry Gottfried.
8. Sander "Sandy" Galton. 9. Will Darnell. 10. Roseanne.

Places   1. Libertyville, Pennsylvania. 2. Libertyville
High School. 3. Darnell's speed shop. 4. Taos, New
Mexico. 5. Barnswallow Drive. 6. Laurel Street. 7. Para-
dise Falls, Ohio. 8. Horlicks. 9. Drew. 10. Monroeville.

Things   1. A red 1958 Plymouth Fury. 2. A Camaro.
3. A Firebird. 4. A 1966 Imperial. 4. A 1975 Duster. 6.
A Mustang. 7. A Valiant. 8. A Hudson Hornet. 9.
97,432.6 miles. 10. A UPS truck.

Quiz 12

People   1. Rachel Creed. 2. Ellie and Gage. 3. Jud
Crandall. 4. Missy Dandridge. 5. Irwin Goldman. 6. Steve
Masterton. 7. Victor Pascow. 8. The Micmacs. 9. Church
(Winston Churchill). 10. Quentin L. Jolander, D.V.M.

Places   1. The Bear's Den. 2. The North Ludlow
Woods. 3. Little God Swamp. 4. Carstairs Street School.
5. The Bangor Holiday Inn. 6. Sing's. 7. The American
Casket Company. 8. Mount Hope Cemetery. 9. The
Greenspan Funeral Home on Fern Street. 10. The
Brookings-Smith Mortuary.

Things   1. A Honda Civic. 2. The Vulture. 3. May 17.
4. The Eternal Rest Casket. 5. "Darvon Day." The day
the drug salesman called on Louis. 6. The file of university students who had physical disabilities. 7. Chester-
field Kings. 8. Spode China. 9. "Sanna." 10. A huge
(and perhaps sentient and malevolent) deadfall.

Quiz 13

People   1. Lily Cavanaugh Sawyer. 2. Speedy Parker. 3. Phil Sawyer. 4. Morgan Sloat. 5. Richard Sloat. 6. Jason DeLoessian. 7. Wolf. 8. Anders. 9. Smokey Updike. 10. Reverend Sunlight Gardener.

Places   1. The Alhambra Inn and Gardens. 2. Point Venuti. 3. The Territories. 4. Thayer School. 5. The Oatley Tunnel. 6. The Blasted Lands. 7. In the black hotel. 8. The Arcadia Funworld. 9. The Queen's Pavillion in the Territories. 10. On the property of the Sunlight Home. It was where most of the boys picked rocks all day.

Things   1. *The Book of Good Farming*. 2. September 1981. 3. She played a "cynical ex-prostitute in a film called *Motorcycle Maniacs*." 4. A white guitar pick. 5. A long tooth, possibly a shark's, inlaid with an intricate pattern of gold. 6. "Right here and now!" 7. Three feet. 8. A black van with "Wild Child" written on its side. 9. A silver coin with Queen Laura DeLoessian's face on it. 10. Uzi submachine guns.

Quiz 14

People   1. The Reverend Lester Lowe. 2. Marty Coslaw. 3. Uncle Al. 4. Arnie Westrum. 5. Milt Sturmfuller. 6. Elmer Zinneman. 7. Mac McCutcheon. 8. Willard Scott. 9. Stan Pelky. 10. Cal Blodwin.

Places   1. Tarker's Mills, Maine. 2. The GS&WM Railroad shack. 3. Ball Street. 4. Forty Acre Field. 5. The Chat 'n Chew. 6. The Commons. 7. The Portland General Hospital Emergency Room. 8. Tarker's Mills Set 'n Sew. 9. The Market Basket. 10. Laurel Street, Tarker's Mills, Maine.

Things   1. An annual April event that had Chris Wrightson as the only participant. 2. "The Beast Walks Among Us." 3. The Reverend Lowe, Baptist Parsonage, Tarker's Mills, Maine 04491. 4. In an electric, battery-powered wheelchair. 5. Camels. 6. The voice Marty's father used when speaking to Marty. 7. A Vulture. 8. The Tarker's Mills Tigers. 9. Marty Coslaw. 10. He was shot with two silver bullets that were made from Marty Coslaw's confirmation spoon.

Quiz 15

People 1. Pennywise the Clown, aka It. 2. Mike Hanlon. 3. Beverly Marsh. 4. Stanley Uris. 5. Dick Hallorann. 6. Eddie Kaspbrak. 7. Richie Tozier. 8. Bill Denbrough. 9. Ben Hanscom. 10. Henry Bowers, Belch Huggins, and Victor Criss.

Places 1. In the Barrens. 2. The house on Neibolt Street. 3. The Standpipe. 4. The Derry Public Library. 5. The Jade of the Orient. 6. The Silver Dollar. 7. The Black Spot. 8. Terrace Park. 9. The Falcon. 10. In the sewers of Derry.

Things 1. Valium, Percodan, Elavil, Darvon Complex, and six Quaaludes in a Sucrets box. 2. Silver. 3. It was a story called "The Dark," and it was published in a magazine called *White Tie*. 4. WZON. 5. Ben Hanscom; Rural Star Route 2; Hemingford Home, Nebraska 59341. 6. Balloons, sometimes with messages from It written on them. 7. The Ritual of Chüd. 8. Beverly Fashions, Inc. 9. Colonel Buford Kissdrivel. 10. His left arm.

Quiz 16

People 1. Roland the Good. 2. His elder son Peter. 3. Sasha. 4. Thomas. 5. Flagg. 6. Niner. 7. Ben Staad. 8. Peony. 9. Quentin Ellender. 10. Aron Beson.

Places 1. The desert of Grenh. 2. The Dismal Swamp. 3. The Hall of the Needle. 4. The Plains of Leng. 5. The Western Barony. 6. Garlan. 7. The Dungeon of Inquisition. 8. In the wall behind the mounted head of Niner the dragon. He watched through the eyes of the dragon. 9. Delain. 10. The Archery Range.

Things 1. The book of spells. 2. A two-headed parrot. 3. An 80 percent tax imposed on the Delain farmers by King Thomas. 4. 1,825 days. 5. The dragon's nine-chambered heart. 6. Roland's father's great arrow. Roland used it to kill Niner the Dragon. 7. Through a sewer outflow pipe. 8. In a triple-locked teak box. 9. He re-

169

moved threads that he later used to make a rope with which to escape. 10. A gold locket and chain, and a note written by Leven Valera.

Quiz 17

People   1. Annie Wilkes. 2. Paul Sheldon. 3. Chastain. 4. Roger Sheldon. 5. Bryce Bell. 6. Tony Bonasaro. 7. Ralph Dugan. 8. Wicks and McKnight. 9. Charlie Merrill. 10. Michael Leith.

Places   1. Wilson's Drug Center. 2. Revere Beach. 3. Riverview Hospital. 4. London's Bedlam Hospital. 5. The Malden Community Center. 6. At the Boulderado Hotel. 7. Ink Beach, Florida. Virginia Sandpiper had turned an upstairs room of her house into Misery's Parlor. 8. Doctors Hospital in Queens. 9. In a new apartment on the East Side of Manhattan. 10. In a deserted East 105th Street tenement.

Things   1. A Red Devil condom. 2. *Misery's Child*. 3. A 1974 Camaro. 4. *Fast Cars*. 5. *Misery's Return*. 6. She used an axe and a Bernz-O-matic torch to cut off his left foot. 7. Novril. 8. They could set the floor at ten million dollars "and then conduct one *hell* of an auction." 9. Hastings House. 10. Royal.

Quiz 18

People   1. Jim Gardener; Gard. 2. Peter. 3. Anne. 4. Joe Paulson. 5. Ron Cummings. 6. Jack Sawyer, of *The Talisman*. 7. David Brown. 8. Ruth McCausland. 9. David Bright. 10. Queenie Golden.

Places   1. Haven, Maine. 2. The old Garrick place. 3. Leighton Street. 4. In Bobbi's shed. 5. Arcadia Beach. 6. Altair-4. 7. A government installation in Virginia called The Shop. 8. In the third-floor corridor of the Haven Town Hall. 9. In the kitchen of her house. 10. In space, on the transparent floor of the control room of the spaceship that had been buried on Bobbi's land.

Things   1. June 21, 1988. 2. It was called *Hangtown*, and it was published in 1975. 3. *Grimoire*. 4. A dozen Eveready alkaline D batteries. 5. The Disappearing

Tomato, the Disappearing Radio, the Disappearing Lawn Chair. 6. *The Buffalo Soldiers*. 7. Cooder's Tavern and Lodging-House. 8. He had a steel plate in his head. 9. *The Upper Room*. 10. The Bangor *Daily News*.

Quiz 19

People   1. George Stark. 2. Alexis Machine. 3. Liz Beaumont. 4. William and Wendy. 5. Rick Cowley. 6. Homer Gamache. 7. Sheriff Alan Pangborn. 8. Dr. Hugh Pritchard. 9. Rawlie DeLesseps. 10. Albert "Fuzzy" Martin.

Places   1. In the Ridgeway section of Bergenfield, New Jersey. 2. Manchester, New Hampshire. 3. Oxford, Mississippi. 4. Oxford, Maine. 5. Homeland Cemetery in Castle Rock, Maine. 6. Fort Laramie, Wyoming. 7. In his Washington, D.C., apartment. 8. Lake Lane. 9. Endsville. 10. The sparrows took him to hell . . . where he belonged.

Things   1. *The Sudden Dancers* and *Purple Haze*. 2. *The Golden Dog*. 3. *Machine's Way, Oxford Blues, Sharkmeat Pie*, and *Riding to Babylon*. 4. The emissaries of the living dead; those who conduct human souls back and forth between the land of the living and the land of the dead. Loons and whippoorwills are outriders of the living; sparrows are outriders of the deceased. 5. "The distant cheeping of a thousand small birds." 6. A straight razor. 7. Berol Black Beauty. 8. *Steel Machine*. 9. "The sparrows are flying again." 10. A black Toronado, and the bumper sticker said HIGH-TONED SON OF A BITCH.

Quiz 20

1. October 2, 1850. 2. "Bones" Granson in Florida. 3. Chapelwaite. 4. Twenty-three. 5. Calvin McCann. 6. Sarah. 7. Mrs. Cloris. 8. *De Vermis Mysteriis*, which translated to *The Mysteries of the Worm*. 9. The *Fence-Rail*. 10. James Robert Boone.

Quiz 21

1. Warwick. 2. Gates Falls. 3. April. 4. The picker machine. 5. Harry Wisconsky. 6. Clean the basement. 7. A

sub-cellar accessible by a trapdoor from the cellar. 8. 1897. 9. The *magna mater*—a queen rat as big as a Holstein calf. 10. Brogan, Ippeston, Dangerfield, Nedeau, and Stevenson.

Quiz 22
1. A6. 2. Corey. 3. Alvin Sackheim. 4. Bernie. 5. Bobby. 6. Susie. 7. Captain Trips. 8. Needles. 9. A2, the Hong Kong flu. 10. In front of the State Theater in Portland. He was doing Leadbelly tunes on a big old Gibson guitar.

Quiz 23
1. Arthur. 2. Project Zeus. 3. Don Lovinger. 4. Richard. 5. Cory. 6. Venus. 7. DESA was the Deep Space Antenna and nine days into the flight it broke and Cory had to go outside to fix it. 8. Cresswell. 9. Dr. Flanders. 10. He grew a perfect circle of twelve golden eyes on his chest.

Quiz 24
1. The Blue Ribbon Laundry. 2. Bill Gartley. 3. A Hadley-Watson Model-6 Speed Ironer and Folder. 4. Adelle Frawley. 5. Officer John Hunton. 6. Mark Jackson. 7. The blood of a virgin, graveyard dirt, hand of glory, bat's blood, night moss, horse's hoof, and eye of toad. 8. Roger Marin. 9. George Stanner. 10. Sherry Ouelette. She cut her hand on one of the clamps.

Quiz 25
1. Dr. Harper. 2. Waterbury, Connecticut. 3. Nurse Vickers. 4. Denny, Andy, and Shirl. 5. Denny died in 1967, Shirl in 1971, and Andy in 1972. 6. Lester's Grammy Ann. 7. Rita. 8. Brain convulsion. 9. Tuesdays and Thursdays. 10. Dr. Harper.

Quiz 26
1. Henry's Nite-Owl. 2. Henry Parmalee. 3. Richie Grenadine. 4. Timmy Grenadine. 5. Dr. Westphail. 6. Golden Light. 7. George Kelso. 8. Rex. 9. Curve Street. 10. Fifty-three seconds.

Quiz 27

1. Cal Bates. 2. $10,000 3. Hans Morris. 4. The Morris Toy Company. 5. Hans Morris's mother. 6. 20 Infantrymen, 10 Helicopters, 2 BAR Men, 2 Bazooka Men, 2 Medics, and 4 Jeeps. They were all alive. 7. A .44 Magnum. 8. *"Surrender."* 9. Ralph and an unnamed girl. (The girl was not supposed to be with Ralph.) 10. 1 Rocket Launcher, 20 Surface-to-air "Twister" Missiles, and 1 Scale-Model Thermonuclear Weapon.

Quiz 28

1. Snodgrass. 2. Conant's Truck Stop & Diner. 3. A 1971 Camaro. 4. Jerry. 5. Pelson. 6. They blew "Attention" with their horns in Morse code, and then "telegraphed" the message, also with their air horns. 7. John Fogarty's "Born on the Bayou." 8. He was run down by a panel truck that had "Wong's Cash-and-Carry Laundry" written on the side. 9. Phillips 66. 10. Two airplanes flying above the truck stop.

Quiz 29

1. Sally. 2. Harold Davis High School. 3. Principal Fenton and Mr. Simmons. 4. Mr. Simmons. 5. Wayne Norman. 6. Vincent Corey, David Garcia, and Robert Lawson. 7. They drove a black 1954 Ford sedan with "Snake Eyes" written on the side. 8. *Raising Demons*. 9. His right and left index fingers. 10. "I'll come back, Jim."

Quiz 30

1. March 16, 1968. 2. New Sharon Teachers' College. 3. Gale Cerman. 4. John Dancey. 5. Her throat was cut. 6. Ann Bray. 7. Her body was propped up behind the wheel of a 1964 Dodge, and parts of her were found in the front and backseats and the trunk. 8. Hanson Gray. 9. Marsha Curran. She was fat and "sadly pretty." 10. The unnamed narrator of the story.

Quiz 31

1. Cressner. 2. 43 stories—400 feet—above the sidewalk. 3. Cressner's wife Marcia. 4. Six ounces of heroin. 5. If Stan Norris successfully walked all the way around the building on the ledge, he got to keep $20,000 cash, and

his lover Marcia. 6. Tony. 7. Five inches. 8. 11:09 P.M. 9. At the morgue. 10. He made Cressner the same wager: He sent him out onto the ledge, and made him walk around the building. Supposedly, if Cressner made it, he was free. But Norris waited for him with a .45. Norris had been known to welsh on a bet.

Quiz 32

1. A silver Lawnboy. 2. Carla Parkette. 3. The Caston-meyer's dog chased it under Harold's lawnmower. 4. Four years old. 5. When her mother was serving either oatmeal for breakfast or spinach for supper. 6. Pastoral Greenery and Outdoor Services. 7. 776-2390. 8. Midwest Bisonburgers, Inc. 9. 1421 East Endicott Street. 10. Sonny.

Quiz 33

1. Jimmy McCann. 2. 29 Maple Lane; Clinton, New York. 3. Alvin Dawes Morrison. 4. Vic Donatti. 5. Lucinda Ramsey Morrison. 6. Mort "Three-Fingers" Minelli. 7. If Dick continued to smoke after punishments one through nine, Step ten was to shoot him and give up. 8. "Stop Going up in Smoke!" 9. $5,000.50 (The 50 cents was for the electricity used to shock his wife in the "rabbit room.") 10. They would cut off his wife's little finger.

Quiz 34

1. A strawberry double-dip ice cream cone. 2. Alice. 3. Professor Branner. 4. 84. 5. Elizabeth's boyfriend, who was killed through voodoo by Ed. 6. The Fifties Stroll trophy. 7. Deedee. 8. *The Golden Bough; Ancient Rites, Modern Mysteries; Haitian Voodoo;* and *The Necronomi-con.* 9. A perfectly rendered "Elizabeth" doll, dressed in a scrap of red nylon; a blue poker chip with a strange red six-sided pattern on it, Mr. and Mrs. Hamner's obituaries (with the same pattern drawn on their faces), one male doll, one female doll, and a red toy Fiat with a piece of Tony Lombard's shirt taped to the front. 10. Her son, Ed, Jr.

Quiz 35

1. Vicky Robeson. 2. He was a medical orderly. 3. Gatlin,

Nebraska. 4. Baby Hortense, an eight-year-old evangelical singer Vicky saw at prayer meetings when she was a child. 5. 25 cents. 6. "The Power and Grace of He Who Walks Behind the Rows." 7. Ruth Clawson. 8. *Cleopatra*. 9. Isaac. 10. Malachi's.

Quiz 36

1. Katrina. He called her Kitty. 2. Wilmington, Delaware. 3. Helen. 4. Hemingford Home, Nebraska, eighty miles west of Omaha. 5. He was a lawyer. 6. Forty-three. 7. Seventy feet. 8. Dr. Pedersen. 9. "Call Girl Swan-Dives To Her Death." 10. "I've been thinking about it a lot lately . . . and what I've decided is it would have been better for me if that last rung had broken before you could put the hay down."

Quiz 37

1. May 1963. 2. New York. 3. Light blue. 4. Norma. 5. Valencia oranges. 6. Ten years. 7. On Seventy-third Street. 8. With a hammer. 9. Five others. The girl in the sailor blouse was his sixth. 10. Love.

Quiz 38

1. Herb Tooklander. 2. Billy Larribee. 3. Booth. 4. Gerard Lumley. 5. New Jersey. 6. Janey Lumley. 7. Francie Lumley. 8. In Jerusalem's Lot. 9. Richie Messina. 10. They were turned into vampires.

Quiz 39

1. Central Maine Hospital in Lewiston. 2. Room 312. 3. Kevin. 4. A cortotomy. 5. Cancer. 6. Sonny's Market. 7. Twenty-two. 8. In Andover, Maine. 9. Six feet, four inches. 10. She died of an overdose of Darvon Complex fed to her by John.

Quiz 40

1. Red, the narrator of the story. 2. Andy Dufresne. 3. Glenn Quentin. 4. Samuel Norton. 5. Andy Dufresne. 6. Zihuatanejo. 7. The "Inside-Out" program. 8. September 15, 1975. 9. May 1950. 10. 1975.

Quiz 41

1. Arthur Denker. 2. Todd Bowden. 3. Andy Dufresne. 4. Foxy. 5. Morris Heisel. 6. Peter's Quality Costume Clothiers. 7. Patin. 8. A nerve gas sent to Dussander at Patin. It made the prisoners leap about screaming and laughing, and it also caused them to vomit and defecate helplessly. Some of Dussander's men called it "Yodeling Gas." 9. A Winchester .30-.30. 10. He committed suicide with an overdose of Seconal.

Quiz 42

1. Chris Chambers, Vern Tessio, Gordie Lachance, and Teddy Duchamp. 2. Ray Brower. 3. Milo Pressman. 4. Chopper. 5. Edward May. 6. Mayor Charbonneau. 7. The Castle River. 8. They were attacked by leeches. 9. Jamie Gallant. 10. Their teacher Mrs. Cote.

Quiz 43

1. Stevens. 2. Dr. Emlyn McCarron. 3. Sandra Stansfield. 4. 249B East Thirty-fifth Street. 5. David Adley. 6. December 23rd, 197-. 7. *These Were Our Brothers*. 8. "It is the tale, not he who tells it." 9. The method of childbirth now known as the Lamaze Method. 10. David Adley's boss. He invited David to The Club the night the story of the Breathing Method was told.

Quiz 44

1. On Long Lake in Maine. 2. Steff. 3. Billy. 4. Brent Norton. 5. Federal Foods Supermarket. 6. Mrs. Carmody. 7. Ambrose Cornell. 8. In a Howard Johnson's near Exit 3 of the Maine Turnpike. 9. Giant, monstrous, mutant insects. 10. They were heading for Hartford, and it sounded like "hope."

Quiz 45

1. Charles. 2. The third grade. 3. Miss Bird. 4. Cathy Scott or Kenny Griffen. 5. Mrs. Trask. 6. A blue Camaro. 7. NIBROC. 8. The Star Theatre. 9. *Roads to Everywhere*. 10. A tiger.

Quiz 46

1. Dennis. 2. Peter ("Petey"). 3. Terry. 4. National

Aerodyne in California. 5. He worked for Texas Instruments at $4,000 less a year. 6. Johnny McCabe. 7. Leonard White. 8. Mrs. Stukey from the helicopter plant. 9. At the bottom of Crystal Lake in Maine. 10. Betsy Moriarty.

Quiz 47
1. Curt. 2 . The Beaver. 3. Rudolph Valentino. 4. It said that Howdy Doody was a pervert. 5. Rollins. 6. Jimmy Brody. 7. Garrish's ex-roommate Pig Pen. 8. A .352 Magnum with a telescopic sight. 9. The Carlton Memorial women's dormitory. 10. A blond coed in jeans and a blue shell top.

Quiz 48
1. Homer Buckland. 2. On Castle Lake, in Castle Rock, Maine. 3. Ophelia Todd ('Phelia). 4. Joe Camber. 5. A Mercedes. A two-seater sportster. 6. Franklin. 7. Motorway B. 8. Bell's Market 9. Vermont. 10. Olympus.

Quiz 49
1. Whitehead City, Mars. 2. Texaco Water. 3. Twelve. 4. Victor Carune. 5. 0.000000000067 of a second. 6. *The Politics of the Jaunt.* 7. The first person to jaunt awake. 8. "It's eternity in there." 9. A button that erased all jaunt emergence portals. 10. "Longer than you think."

Quiz 50
1. Mike Scollay. 2. Tommy Englander. 3. Two C's. (Two hundred dollars.) 4. The Sons of Erin Hall on Grover Street. 5. Billy-Boy Williams. 6. Maureen and Rico Romano. 7. Miss Gibson. 8. Demetrius Katzenos. 9. She stuck a piece of piano wire through his left eye into his brain while he knelt before her. 10. She died of a heart attack in 1933 and some of the papers said she weighed five hundred pounds.

Quiz 51
1. In Cascade Lake. 2. Horlicks University in Pittsburgh. 3. A Camaro. 4. Randy. 5. Rachel. 6. LaVerne. 7. Rachel. 8. Deke. 9. LaVerne. 10. The lead singer of AC/DC who had puked down his own throat and died.

Quiz 52

1. Jonathan Hagstrom. 2. Seth. 3. Bernie Epstein. 4. Mr. Nordhoff. 5. Roger. 6. A Fender. 7. His wife's photograph. 8. At Our Lady of Perpetual Sorrows Church. 9. Father Phillips. 10. "I am a man who lives alone except for my wife, Belinda, and my son, Jonathan."

Quiz 53

1. Stevens. 2. 249B East 35th Street. 3. George Gregson. 4. Eighty-five. 5. He lived in rooms on Brennan Street, and he had been living there since 1919. 6. Henry Brower. 7. Darrel Baker. 8. Jason Davidson. 9. Bombay. 10. He died by shaking his own hand.

Quiz 54

1. FedShip ASN/29. 2. Grimes. 3. Shapiro. 4. CL. #23196755. 5. The Beach Boys. 6. A belt trader. 7. Dud. 8. Gomez. 9. Excellent Montoya. 10. Fourteen years.

Quiz 55

1. The Delver looking-glass. 2. The Samuel Claggert Memorial Private Museum. 3. Mr. Carlin. 4. $250,000. 5. Johnson Spangler. 6. With a rock. 7. An unnamed English duchess. 8. An unnamed Pennsylvania rug merchant. 9. John Delver; England's Elizabethan period. 10. A hooded figure; The Reaper; Death.

Quiz 56

1. "Do you love?" 2. Joe's Good Eats. 3. The Eye. 4. Norman Blanchette. 5. Cheryl Craig. 6. Hollis. 7. Ace Merrill. 8. Emonds. He lived on Bowen Hill. 9. Curt. 10. His name was Drake and he died in a house fire when the narrator was in the hospital with the flu.

Quiz 57

1. January 24th. 2. 190 paces wide, by 267 paces long. 3. Richard Pinzetti. 4. Steinbrunner, the Jew grocer. 5. He had two kilos of pure heroin worth $350,000. 6. Henry Li-Tsu. 7. Ronnie Hannelli, the man who gave Pine the big Chink's name. 8. His right foot. 9. A dead fish, "rotten and stinking." 10. His fingers. "Lady fingers they taste just like lady fingers."

Quiz 58

1. 1905. 2. Derry, Maine. 3. George McCutcheon. 4. Billy Dodd. 5. It was on Route 117, and it had previously been the Castle Ridge School. 6. It was willed to the University of Maine Forestry Department. 7. His nephew Quentin. 8. Diamond Gem Oil. 9. Carl Durkin. 10. A Maxi-Duty Champion spark plug.

Quiz 59

1. The Mackenzies. 2. Cramer's Dairy. 3. Spike. 4. Rocky. 5. A tarantula in an empty chocolate milk carton. 6. A bottle of all-purpose cream filled with an acid gel. 7. A carton of eggnog spiked with belladonna. 8. The Kincaids. 9. Two quarts of milk and a pint of whipping cream. It was not said if they were "spiked." 10. A clump of hair and a few splinters of bone.

Quiz 60

1. A 1957 Chrysler. 2. Leo. 3. The New Adams Laundry. 4. Four months. 5. Spike Milligan, the milkman. 6. Fifteen dollars a week. 7. Bob Driscoll. 8. "Stiff Socks." 9. Laundry wheels. 10. The torture-murder of a young girl and her boyfriend there in 1968. Their body parts were found throughout the boyfriend's 1959 Mercury. That same car later did away with Rocky and Leo, thanks to Spike Milligan, the milkman, who was also more than likely the murderer of the two kids in 1968.

Quiz 61

1. Ruth. 2. Buddy. 3. Dr. Arlinder, and his phone number was 681-4330. 4. The Spoon Torture of the Heathen Chinee and Indian Rope Burns. 5. Heather MacArdle. 6. The Tigers. 7. Henrietta Dodd. 8. Uncle Franklin. 9. Joe Camber's hill. 10. She told him to tell her to "Lie down in the Name of Hastur."

Quiz 62

1. The poet Marianne Moore. 2. "The Ballad of the Flexible Bullet." 3. *Underworld Figures*. 4. Henry Wilson. 5. "Fornit Some Fornus." 6. Luck-elves that lived in Reg Thorpe's typewriter. 7. Good-luck dust that the Fornits shot from guns. 8. Rackne. 9. Andy Rivers. 10. Jimmy Rulin.

Quiz 63

1. November 19, 1884. 2. Goat Island. 3. At the Goat Island Store. 4. "A body of water between two bodies of land, a body of water which is open at either end." 5. The Reverend Ewell McCracken. 6. Her dead husband Bill Flanders. 7. 1958. 8. George Dinsmore. 9. Her dead husband Bill's cap. 10. "On those long nights alone, with his mother Stella Flanders at long last in her grave, it often seemed to Alden that they did both." (Although a simple "yes" will more than adequately suffice.)

Quiz 64

1. The house was "an architectural monstrosity." 2. Barney. 3. "There's one born every minute." 4. Carmen's Folly. 5. $180,000. 6. Cappy MacFarland. 7. Jagger's. 8. The Sarge. 9. An "ancient" Videomaster tv. 10. In the base of a lamp.

Quiz 65

1. Teaching. 2. Emily. 3. "Vacation." 4. Robert. 5. Mr. Hanning. 6. Margaret Crossen. 7. Jim Sidley. 8. The mimeograph room. 9. The Summer Street School. 10. Buddy Jenkins.

Quiz 66

1. John Halston. 2. Halston had killed eighteen men and six women. 3. Drogan. 4. Saul Loggia. 5. The synthetic drug Tri-Dormal-phenobarbin, compound G. It was a painkiller, tranquilizer, and mild hallucinogen that had been developed in the fifties. 6. Amanda Drogan. 7. Carolyn Broadmoor. 8. Dick Gage. 9. A 1973 Plymouth with a custom Cyclone Spoiler engine, a Pensy shift, Hearst linkage, and Bobby Unser Wide Oval tires. 10. First the cat attacked him, causing him to ditch his car. The cat then wormed its way into Halston's mouth, crawled all the way down his throat into his stomach, and then ate his way out of Halston's body.

Quiz 67

1. Mr. Legere. 2. Green Terror. 3. Jason Indrasil. 4. Eddie Johnston. 5. The Farnum & Williams' All-American 3-Ring Circus and Side Show. 6. Sally O'Hara. 7. Andrea

Solienni. 8. "The Demon Cat Cage." 9. Kelly Nixon and Mike McGregor. 10. Ebony Velvet.

Quiz 68
1. PC Ted Vetter and PC Robert Farnham. 2. Tottenham Lane. 3. Lonnie Freeman. 4. Danny and Norma. 5. Sergeant Sid Raymond. 6. John Squales. 7. In the Brass End section of London. 8. A deserted warehouse. 9. On the Ford assembly line. 10. August 19, 1974.

Quiz 69
1. James Parris. 2. Boyd. 3. Lottie Kilgallon. 4. William Pillsbury. 5. Lewis Toner. 6. 259 pounds. 7. His father kicked him out of the treehouse. 8. Tony Giorgio. 9. Walt Abruzzi. 10. The dead.

Quiz 70
1. Elizabeth Robinson. 2. The Ninth Street Health Club. 3. Harvey Blocker. 4. Tinker. 5. Big Joe's Cleaning Service. 6. Twenty rull. 7. "Not quite five feet wide by forty-two feet long." 8. $55,000. 9. A 1968 Chevrolet. 10. Three slipped discs and a serious lower spinal dislocation.

Quiz 71
1. Placerville High School. 2. Mrs. Underwood. 3. Thomas Denver. 4. John Carlson. 5. Mr. Grace. 6. Peter Franklin. 7. Frank Philbrick. 8. Ted Jones. 9. (Judge) Samuel K. N. Deleavney. 10. His high school yearbook.

Quiz 72
1. Ray Garraty. 2 . The Major. 3. Three. If a Walker was warned a fourth time, he was shot. 4. Seven and three-quarter miles. 5. 47. 6. The Maine/Canada border. 7. May 1st, at 9:00 A.M. 8. The Major's Bedlington terrier. 9. Jan. 10. "Save your wind. If you smoke ordinarily, try not to smoke on the Long Walk."

Quiz 73
1. November 20, 1973. 2. Harold Swinnerton. 3. Mary. 4. The Blue Ribbon Laundry. 5. He died of an inoperable brain tumor. 6. The 784 extension. 7. Southern Com-

fort and Seven-Up. 8. Olivia. 9. He lived at 1241 Crestallen Street West. 10. "Dawes' Last Stand."

Quiz 74
1. Sheila. 2. Cathy. 3. Co-Op City. 4. Free-Vee. 5. Blams. 6. Dan Killian. 7. *Treadmill to Bucks*. 8. Dokes. 9. The Network Games Building. 10. John Griffen Springer.

Quiz 75
1. Susanna Lemke. 2. His wife was Heidi; his daughter Linda. 3. Taduz Lemke. 4. Greely, Penschley, Kinder, and Halleck. 5. Richard Ginelli. 6. Three Brothers restaurant. 7. Fairview, Connecticut. 8. 246 pounds. 9. A mixture of Mexican brown heroin and strychnine that Richard Ginelli injected into steaks and then fed to Taduz Lemke's pit bulls. 10. Billy had to cut his hand and put his blood into what looked like a strawberry pie given to him by Taduz Lemke. The only catch was that Billy had to make someone else eat the pie or the curse would return. Without his knowing it, his wife and daughter each ate a piece of the pie, thereby giving Lemke his final revenge.

Quiz 76
1. Two. 2. He was at the fifth level. 3. The man in black. 4. Brown. 5. Zoltan. 6. Pappa Doc. 7. Tull. 8. In the High Speech. 9. Alice ("Allie.") 10. Sylvia Pittston.

Quiz 77
1. Roland. 2. His mother. (Although at first, the text mistakenly says it was his father.) 3. John Chambers; Jake. 4. He twirled one of the shells from his gunbelt. 5. Mrs. Greta Shaw. 6. He was pushed beneath the wheels of a blue 1976 Cadillac. 7. A speaking-demon with the voice of Alice from Tull. 8. A jawbone, rotted at the far hinge. 9. Cuthbert. 10. Cort.

Quiz 78
1. Susan. 2. She was burned to death before Roland's eyes. 3. The Speaking Demon jawbone and the forked finger gesture. 4. Mescaline. 5. Heroin. 6. The boy. 7.

New Canaan. 8. Hax. 9. Wearing a hooded robe and holding a staff, his hand held out in a "mocking gesture" of welcome. 10. Three.

Quiz 79
1. The Hall of Grandfathers. 2. Marten. 3. Railroad tracks. 4. David, the hawk. 5. "Wait." 6. By putting rocks on the railroad tracks. 7. "Track 10 to Surface and Points West." 8. A bow and a quiver of badly weighted arrows. 9. "Go then. There are other worlds than these." 10. Twelve.

Quiz 80
1. A rabbit. 2. Jerky. He feared enchanted meat. 3. The Hanged Man, the Sailor, the Prisoner, the Lady of Shadows, Death, the Tower, and Life. 4. The universe. 5. The Mohaine Desert. 6. The Ageless Stranger. His name was Maerlyn. 7. The Beast. 8. Walter. 9. Ten years. 10. The Tower.

Quiz 81
1. Lobstrosities. 2. Eddie Dean. 3. Henry Dean. 4. Johnny Cash. (Yes, we all know the *actual* correct answer is *The Exorcist*, but Henry Dean answered "Johnny Cash" to everything and so we must count that as the correct answer. This question was asked during a game of Trivial Pursuit between Henry and George Biondi.) 5. Odetta Holmes and Detta Walker. 6. Andrew Feeny. 7. Jack Mort. 8. Fat Johnny Holden. 9. Susannah Dean. 10. The third is called *The Waste Lands*, the fourth is *Wizard and Glass*.

Quiz 82
1. The Granthams. 2. Aunt Sylvia. 3. Cassandra. 4. Aunt Bedelia. 5. She supposedly killed her father with an ashtray. 6. Aunt Bedelia's fiance. 7. Her father had him killed in a "hunting accident." 8. Nathan Grantham. 9. Mrs. Danvers. 10. Richard.

Quiz 83
1. The local college's "Department of Meteors." 2. $50. 3. $200. 4. Mr. Bilkmore. 5. The Reverend Fleece U.

White. 6. The Church of the Holy Shrinking Purse. 7. Doc Geeson. 8. Dr. Peter V. Higgins of Castle Rock.

"Weeds" Answers: 9. Plain thinking, work thinking, and Big Thinking. Big Thinking included such things as what he would do if all the cows died, what bills to pay at the end of the month, and what to do with the meteor. 10. The seed catalogues, Louis L'Amour westerns, and dirty books.

Quiz 84

1. Horlicks University. 2. Amberson Hall. 3. Under a stairway. 4. A quarter. 5. Mike Latimer. 6. Professor Dexter Stanley. 7. Wilma Northrup.

"The Crate" Answers: 8. Badlinger. 9. Professor Viney. 10. A Zippo.

Quiz 85

1. Harry Wentworth. 2. Richard Vickers. 3. He buried her in the sand on the beach up to her head. 4. He buried him in the sand on the beach up to his head. 5. He set up a video monitor that showed Becky buried in the sand. 6. The bodies of Harry and Becky. 7. *The Bank Dick.* 8. The waterlogged corpses of Harry and Becky. 9. They buried him in the sand on the beach up to his head. 10. The footprints of Harry's and Becky's corpses walking back into the sea.

Quiz 86

1. Upson Pratt. 2. "Cleanliness is next to Prattliness." 3. A black guy named White. 4. Norman Castonmeyer. 5. George Gendron. 6. Carl Reynolds. 7. The Parelli Brothers. 8. In the projects. 9. Sergeant Meggs. 10. He was physically invaded by cockroaches.

Quiz 87

1. Inspector Lestrade. 2. 221B Baker Street. 3. Mrs. Hudson. 4. Saville Row. 5. Mr. Barnes. 6. Mr. Oliver Stanley. 7. William, Jory, and Stephen. 8. Lady Rebecca Hull. 9. 300,000 pounds. 10. His son Jory Hull.

Quiz 88

1. Briggs Sheridan. 2. The Cousintown Mall. 3. Mr. Wizard. 4. The Pittsburgh Penguins. 5. $35,000. 6. His Popsy. 7. McDonald's. 8. Twenty years in Hammerton Bay. 9. Ted Lapidus. 10. Popsy slit his throat and let the kid drink Sheridan's blood.

Quiz 89

1. November 30, 1989. 2. Edward Paladin. 3. Albert K. Dellums. 4. Detective 2nd Grade Pete Jacoby and Detective 1st Grade Richard Cheyney. 5. "You don't shit where you eat." 6. Joan Raiford. 7. Lieutenant McEachern. 8. Red. 9. Salmon pink. 10. James Madison.

Quiz 90

1. Tabori Studios. 2. Under the door of the first stall of the third floor men's room. 3. Paul Janning. 4. The Dead Beats. 5. "Diving in the Dirt." 6. Camels. 7. The Satin Saturns. 8. McManus's Pub. 9. Somebody stuck a yellow Eberhard Faber #2 pencil in his eye. 10. Cartin's.

Quiz 91

1. Le Palais. 2. Peter Rosewall. 3. Delores Williams. 4. *Blaze of Glory*. 5. Harvey Williams. 6. Mama Delorme. 7. Novelist Peter Jeffries. 8. 1946. 9. Bradford. 10. *Boys in the Mist*.

Quiz 92

1. *Inside View*. 2. Merton Morrison. 3. Melanie Briggs. 4. N101BL. 5. *Inside View* and Stephen King. 6. Gloria Swett. 7. Ezra. 8. Dwight Renfield. 9. The psychic Johnny Smith. 10. *The Vampire Lestat* by Anne Rice.

Quiz 93

1. George Banning. 2. Clivey Banning. 3. Troy, New York. The West Orchard. 4. "Use it, use it, and don't, for heaven's sake, ever dare to lose it! Keep it up! Use it up! Break it in, and never pout! Do it in or do without!" 5. Arthur Osgood. 6. A tarnished silver pocket watch. 7. Time. 8. Johnny Brinkmayer. 9. Reverend Toddman. 10. "[H]aving a pony to ride was better than having no pony at all, no matter how the weather of its heart might lie."

Quiz 94

1. Willow, Maine. 2. John and Elise Graham. 3. The University of Missouri. 4. The Hempstead Place. 5. Henry Eden. 6. Laura Stanton. 7. The rainy season took place every seven years on the evening of June 17th. 8. It rained toads. 9. Lucy Ducet. 10. They were eaten by vicious, fanged toads when the coal-chute burst open and flooded their basement hiding place.

Quiz 95

1. Jack. 2. Maddie Sullivan. 3. Reverend Tom Peebles. 4. Deer Isle, off the coast of Maine. 5. Star Wormwood. 6. "Dead Come to Life in Small Florida Town!" 7. Burt Dorfman. 8. By chopping them up and setting the parts on fire. 9. Frank Daggett. 10. The Pulsifers.

Quiz 96

1. *'Salem's Lot* 2. "The Star Invaders" 3. "Battleground" 4. *Christine* 5. *The Dark Half* 6. "The Man Who Would Not Shake Hands" 7. *Carrie* 8. *The Plant* 9. *The Tommyknockers* 10. *Thinner* 11. *Firestarter* 12. "Rita Hayworth and Shawshank Redemption" 13. *The Dead Zone* 14. *The Shining* 15. "Before the Play"

Quiz 97

1. (b) Chris Hargensen (*Carrie*) 2. (a) Leigh Cabot (*Christine*) 3. (b) Queen Sasha (*The Eyes of the Dragon*) 4. (c) Ellie (*Pet Sematary*) 5. (a) Charity (*Cujo*) 6. (b) Patricia McCardle (*The Tommyknockers*) 7. (a) Bobbi Anderson (*The Tommyknockers*) 8. (b) Patty Oates ("The Jaunt," *Skeleton Crew*) 9. (b) Bev Rogan (*It*) 10. (b) Sue Norton (*'Salem's Lot*) 11. (a) Mrs. Underwood (*Rage*) 12. (c) Jane ("Stud City," from "The Body," *Different Seasons*) 13. (c) Vicky (*Firestarter*) 14. (b) Vera (*The Dead Zone*) 15. (a) Mother Abagail (*The Stand*)

Quiz 98

1. (a) Greg Stillson (*The Dead Zone*) 2. (b) Irv Manders (*Firestarter*) 3. (c) Ian Carmichael (*Misery's Return*) 4. (c) Andy Dufresne ("Rita Hayworth and Shawshank Redemption") 5. (a) Herman Coslaw (*Cycle of the Werewolf*) 6. (b) Jimmy McCann ("Quitters, Inc.") 7.

(a) George Hatfield (*The Shining*) 8. (b) Stebbins (*The Long Walk*) 9. (c) Jessie Rider (*The Stand*) 10. (c) Ben Hanscom (*It*) 11. (a) Matt Burke (*'Salem's Lot*) 12. (b) Johnny Renshaw ("Battleground") 13. (b) Richard Dees ("The Night Flier") 14. (a) Roger Breakstone (*Cujo*) 15. (c) Robertson Davies (*The Tommyknockers*)

Quiz 99

1. New Sharon Teachers' College	I. "Strawberry Spring"
2. Acorn Street Grammar School.	A. "Here There Be Tygers"
3. Ewen High School	H. *Carrie*
4. Horlicks University	E. "The Raft"
5. Harold Davis High School	G. "Sometimes They Come Back"
6. Libertyville High School	F. *Christine*
7. Thayer School	J. *The Talisman*
8. Summer Street School	B. "Suffer the Little Children"
9. Cleaves Mills High School	D. *The Dead Zone*
10. Placerville High School	C. *Rage*

Quiz 100

1. A haunted hotel—H. *The Shining* 2. Vampires—V. *'Salem's Lot*, GG. "One for the Road," TT. "The Night Flier" 3. A single, psychopathic teenager—A. *Rage* 4. The Boogeyman—N. "The Boogeyman" 5. A haunted amusement park—YY. "Skybar" 6. The Mummy—C. *It* 7. A teenage voodoo expert—S. "I Know What You Need" 8. A demonic shirt folding machine—L. "The Mangler" 9. A malicious, sadistic millionaire—R. "The Ledge" 10. Living, vengeful toy soldiers—B. "Battleground" 11. Spoiled beer—K. "Gray Matter" 12. Ghosts—P. "Sometimes They Come Back" 13. Modern medicine—EE. "The Woman in the Room" 14. A killer flu—I. "Night Surf," ZZ. *The Stand* 15. The government—E. *The Long Walk* 16. Zombies—VV. "Home Delivery" 17. A house that grows by itself—FF. "It Grows On You" 18. Living, malevolent trucks—D. "Trucks" 19. A cat from Hell—DD. "The Cat from Hell" 20. A man

who steals children—XX. "Popsy" 21. A haunted toilet stall—LL. "Sneakers" 22. The Wolfman—C. *It* 23. Giant mutant rats—F. "Graveyard Shift" 24. A psychopathic, schizophrenic serial killer—T. "Strawberry Spring" 25. A corn God—Y. "Children of the Corn" 26. A rabid St. Bernard—CC. *Cujo* 27. Unwanted precognitive abilities—HH. *The Dead Zone* 28. A mad scientist—X. "I Was a Teenage Grave Robber" 29. Unwanted pyrokinetic abilities—AA. *Firestarter* 30. The Wendigo—Q. *Pet Sematary* 31. A giant alien spider—C. *It* 32. A beautiful dead ghost—M. "Nona" 33. Slow Mutants—II. *The Dark Tower: The Gunslinger* 34. A dead grandmother—W. "Gramma" 35. A Werewolf—OO. *Cycle of the Werewolf* 36. Evil Twinners—NN. *The Talisman* 37. A haunted mirror—PP. "The Reaper's Image" 38. An evil wizard—BB. *The Eyes of the Dragon* 39. Leeches—RR. "The Body" 40. A Gypsy curse—QQ. *Thinner* 41. A killer nurse—Z. *Misery* 42. A mist—O. "The Mist" 43. The monster in the water—SS. "The Raft" 44. A desert island—U. "Survivor Type" 45. A living planet—JJ. "Beachworld" 46. Aliens—G. "I Am The Doorway," J. *The Tommyknockers* 47. Plants from Hell—WW. *The Plant* 48. Time—MM. "My Pretty Pony" 49. A haunted glass floor—KK. "The Glass Floor" 50. Demonic grammar school children—UU. "Suffer the Little Children

Quiz 101

1. Solarcaine. (*Firestarter*) 2. Black Forest. (*Carrie*) 3. Campbell's Chunky Beef. (*Christine*) 4. Chivas Regal. (*The Dead Zone*) 5. Calo. (*Pet Sematary*) 6. Gelusil. (*Cujo*) 7. *Newsweek.* ("Rita Hayworth and Shawshank Redemption") 8. Twinkies. (*Thinner*) 9. Iron City. ("Big Wheels: A Tale of The Laundry Game [Milkman #2]") 10. Za-Rex. ("The Reach") 11. Gulf. (*It*) 12. Kools. ("Apt Pupil") 13. Coke. (*The Tommyknockers*) 14. Table Talk. (*The Shining*) 15. Dr. Pepper. ("The Breathing Method") 16. Darvon Complex. (*"The Woman in the Room"*) 17. Betadine. (*Misery*) 18. Fisher-Price. (*The Stand*) 19. Rollos. ("The Body") 20. Kentucky Fried Chicken. (*The Talisman*)

Quiz 102

1. Sissy Spacek—F. *CARRIE* 2. Rob Reiner—K. *STAND BY ME* 3. Jack Nicholson—L. *THE SHINING* 4. Heather Locklear—G. *FIRESTARTER* 5. Tobe Hooper—M. *'SALEM'S LOT* 6. Denise Crosby—D. *PET SEMATARY* 7. Stephen King—A. *CREEPSHOW* 8. Emilio Estevez—O. *MAXIMUM OVERDRIVE* 9. Candy Clark—I. *CAT'S EYE* 10. Linda Hamilton—C. *CHILDREN OF THE CORN* 11. Harry Dean Stanton—B. *CHRISTINE* 12. Dee Wallace—N. *CUJO* 13. Gary Busey—H. *SILVER BULLET* 14. Christopher Walken—J. *THE DEAD ZONE* 15. Arnold Schwarzenegger—E. *THE RUNNING MAN*

Quiz 103

1. Bob Gray—S. *It* 2. Bobbi Anderson—P. *The Tommyknockers* 3. Jud Crandall—D. *Pet Sematary* 4. John Rainbird—N. *Firestarter* 5. Charles Decker—H. *Rage* 6. Mark Petrie—O. *'Salem's Lot* 7. Mrs. Carmody—L. "The Mist" 8. Zoltan—T. "The Gunslinger" 9. Marty Coslaw—M. *Cycle of the Werewolf* 10. Paul Sheldon—B. *Misery* 11. Larry Underwood—G. *The Stand* 12. Ophelia Todd—A. "Mrs. Todd's Shortcut" 13. Hal Shelburn—E. "The Monkey" 14. Carlos Detweiller—C. *The Plant* 15. Charles Boone—F. "Jerusalem's Lot" 16. Barton Dawes—R. *Roadwork* 17. Detta Walker/Odetta Holmes—K. *The Drawing of the Three* 18. Sherlock Holmes—J. "The Doctor's Case" 19. Kurt Dussander—Q. "Apt Pupil" 20. Wolf—I. *The Talisman*

Quiz 104

1. Milo Pressman, "The Body," *Different Seasons* 2. Carrie White, *Carrie* 3. Dr. Joseph Wanless, *Firestarter* 4. Lloyd the bartender, *The Shining* 5. Jim Gardener, *The Tommyknockers* 6. Will Darnell, *Christine* 7. The Sharp Cereal Professor, *Cujo* 8. Annie Wilkes, *Misery* 9. The speaking-demon, *The Dark Tower: The Gunslinger*; "The Way Station" 10. Bill Denbrough, *It*

Quiz 105

1. FALSE. It was Bobbi Anderson. 2. TRUE. He had published short stories. 3. FALSE. It was Ad Worx. 4.

TRUE. 5. FALSE. It was Stan Uris who killed himself. 6. TRUE. She sure was. 7. FALSE. He died when Flagg ignited the atomic bomb Trash had in the back of his electric cart. 8. FALSE. The town was in Maine. 9. TRUE. 10. FALSE. She went to *Rolling Stone*. (Give yourself half credit if you said "True" based on the film. But we are talking about the books here!) 11. FALSE. He broke it open and it turned him and his farm into a jungle. 12. TRUE. 13. TRUE. 14. FALSE. He drove a Cadillac. 15. FALSE. It was a taxi accident. (Once again, take half a point if you said "True" based on the movie.) 16. FALSE. He wrote for *Inside View*. 17. FALSE. It was a Berol Black Beauty pencil. 18. TRUE. 19. FALSE. He was a contestant on *The Running Man*. 20. FALSE. It was the right.

Quiz 106

1-K-GG 2-J-SS 3-N-FF 4-D-KK 5-L-LL 6-G-EE 7-A-CC
8-Q-AA 9-P-OO 10-F-PP 11-S-HH 12-B-NN 13-R-MM
14-C-QQ 15-H-BB 16-E-RR 17-I-JJ 18-M-II 19-T-II
20-O-DD

Quiz 107

1. In a lead-lined vault in Paris. The notebooks are too radioactive to touch. (*The Tommyknockers*, p. 75, hardcover edition.) 2. The Connecticut Union Bank. (*Thinner*, p. 99, hardcover edition.) 3. Steve Kemp. (*Cujo*, p. 261, hardcover edition.) 4. Chicken. (*The Drawing of the Three*, p. 165, hardcover edition.) 5. "Aunt Hagar's Blues." ("The Wedding Gig," *Skeleton Crew*, p. 227, hardcover edition.) 6. "The earth is taken: this is not your home." (Karl Shapiro, "Travelogue for Exile," epigraph to Part 5 of *It*, "The Ritual of Chüd," p. 895, hardcover edition.) 7. Biffer. (*Pet Sematary*, p. 29, hardcover edition.) 8. H. P. Lovecraft. ("Crouch End," in *The Dark Descent*, p. 692, hardcover edition. See Bibliography.) 9. "Why do I feel so all alone?" (*Carrie*, p. 72, paperback edition.) 10. Edwin. (Okay, I lied.)

A STEPHEN KING BIBLIOGRAPHY:

Part One: Novels and Collections

This Bibliography is in two parts: *Novels and Collections*, and *Short Stories and Novellas*.

For the novels and collections, I've listed those editions of the works that I felt were the most accessible and would be the easiest to find. I've omitted the limited editions since you're probably not going to go out and buy a $400 copy of *The Gunslinger* when the NAL trade paperback can be had for $10.95. Following this line of reasoning, I also omitted bibliographic information for the original Signet editions of Richard Bachman's novels. These are now collector's items, and are priced accordingly. All you need to answer the quiz questions is the NAL paperback edition of these novels, and so these mass-market volumes are the books I chose to include here.

The Short Story and Novellas bibliography is not the complete listing of Stephen King's shorter works. It consists of the works included in *The Stephen King Quiz Book* as quiz subjects (or stories referred to in the book), and it lists, once again, what I felt were the easiest to find.

When trying to track down these tales, don't overlook your local public library. Many of the anthologies listed are available in libraries, and if your local library doesn't have it, they can often get a copy of the book through an interlibrary loan. (My local New Haven library did not have *The Evil Image: Two Centuries of Gothic Short Fiction and Poetry* containing "Suffer the Little Children," but a number of other Connecticut libraries did, and I had it within a few days. Interestingly, I recently found a copy of the out-of-print *Playboy* paperback

Nightmares—a volume that also contained "Suffer the Little Children"—in a used bookstore in my area. They were asking twenty-five cents for it. Used bookstores are often a goldmine for this kind of stuff and should not be overlooked either.)

•*The Bachman Books*
  Hardcover: New York: New American Library, NAL Books, 1985.
  Trade paperback: New York: New American Library, Plume, 1985.
  Paperback: New York: New American Library, Signet, 1986.

• *Carrie*
  Hardcover: Garden City, NY: Doubleday, 1974.
  Paperback: New York: New American Library, Signet, 1975.

• *Christine*
  Hardcover: New York: Viking, 1983.
  Paperback: New York: New American Library, Signet, 1984.

• *Creepshow*
  Trade Paperback: New York: New American Library, Plume, 1982.

Cujo
  Hardcover: New York: Viking, 1981.
  Paperback: New York: New American Library, Signet, 1982.

• *Cycle of the Werewolf*
  Trade Paperback: New York: New American Library, Plume, 1985.

• *The Dark Half*
  Hardcover: New York: Viking, 1989.
  Paperback: New York: New American Library, Signet, 1990.

• *The Dark Tower: The Gunslinger*
  Trade Paperback: New York: New American Library, Plume, 1988.

- *The Dark Tower II: The Drawing of the Three*
  Trade Paperback: New York: New American Library, Plume, 1989.

- *The Dead Zone*
  Hardcover: New York: Viking, 1979.
  Paperback: New York: New American Library, Signet, 1980.

- *Different Seasons*
  Hardcover: New York: Viking, 1982.
  Paperback: New York: New American Library, Signet, 1983.

- *The Eyes of the Dragon*
  Hardcover: New York: Viking, 1987.
  Paperback: New York: New American Library, Signet, 1988.

- *Firestarter*
  Hardcover: New York: Viking, 1980.
  Paperback: New York: New American Library, Signet, 1981.

- *It*
  Hardcover: New York: Viking, 1986.
  Paperback: New York: New American Library, Signet, 1987.

- *The Long Walk* (in *The Bachman Books*)
  Trade paperback: New York: New American Library, Plume, 1985.
  Paperback: New York: New American Library, Signet, 1986.

- *Misery*
  Hardcover: New York: Viking, 1987.
  Paperback: New York: New American Library, Signet, 1988.

- *Night Shift*
  Hardcover: Garden City, NY: Doubleday, 1978.
  Paperback: New York: New American Library, Signet, 1979.

- *Pet Sematary*
  Hardcover: Garden City, NY: Doubleday, 1983.
  Paperback: New York: New American Library, Signet, 1984.

- *Rage* (in *The Bachman Books*)
  Trade paperback: New York: New American Library, Plume, 1985.
  Paperback: New York: New American Library, Signet, 1986.

- *Roadwork* (in *The Bachman Books*)
  Trade paperback: New York: New American Library, Plume, 1985.
  Paperback: New York: New American Library, Signet, 1986.

- *The Running Man* (in *The Bachman Books*)
  Trade paperback: New York: New American Library, Plume, 1985.
  Paperback: New York: New American Library, Signet, 1986.

- *'Salem's Lot*
  Hardcover: Garden City, NY: Doubleday, 1975.
  Paperback: New York: New American Library, Signet, 1978.

- *The Shining*
  Hardcover: Garden City, NY: Doubleday, 1977.
  Paperback: New York: New American Library, Signet, 1978.

- *Skeleton Crew*
  Hardcover: New York: Putnam, 1985.
  Paperback: New York: New American Library, Signet, 1986.

- *The Stand*
  Hardcover: Garden City, NY: Doubleday, 1978.
  Paperback: New York: New American Library, Signet, 1979.

- *The Stand: The Complete & Uncut Edition*
  Hardcover: Garden City, NY: Doubleday, 1990.

- *The Talisman* (with Peter Straub)
  Hardcover: New York: Viking and Putnam, 1984.
  Paperback: New York: Berkley, 1985.

- *Thinner* (as Richard Bachman)
  Hardcover: New York: New American Library, NAL Books, 1984.
  Paperback: New York: New American Library, Signet, 1985.

- *The Tommyknockers*
  Hardcover: New York: Putnam, 1987.
  Paperback: New York: New American Library, Signet, 1988.

Part Two: Short Stories and Novellas

- "Apt Pupil"
  Different Seasons, 1982

- "The Ballad of the Flexible Bullet"
  Skeleton Crew, 1985.

- "Battleground"
  Night Shift, 1978.

- "Beachworld"
  Skeleton Crew, 1985.

- "Before the Play"
  1. *Whispers*, August 1982.
  2. *The Shape Under the Sheet: The Complete Stephen King Encyclopedia* by Stephen J. Spignesi (Popular Culture, Ink. 1990).

- "Big Wheels: A Tale of the Laundry Game (Milkman #2)"
  Skeleton Crew, 1985.

- "The Body"
  Different Seasons, 1982.

- "The Boogeyman"
  Night Shift, 1978.

- "The Breathing Method"
  Different Seasons, 1982.

- "Cain Rose Up"
  Skeleton Crew, 1985.

- "The Cat from Hell"
  1. *Cavalier*, June 1977.
  2. *The Year's Finest Fantasy.* Ed. Terry Carr (Berkley paperback, 1979).
  3. *Magicats!* Ed. Jack Dann and Gardner Dozois (Ace paperback, 1984).

- "Children of the Corn"
  Night Shift, 1978.

- "The Crate"
  Creepshow, 1982.

- "Crouch End"
  1. *New Tales of the Cthulhu Mythos.* Ed. Ramsey Campbell (Arkham House hardcover, 1980).
  2. *The Dark Descent.* Ed. David G. Hartwell (Tor hardcover, 1987).

- "Dedication"
  Night Visions 5. Ed. Douglas E. Winter (Dark Harvest, 1988).

- "The Doctor's Case"
  The New Adventures of Sherlock Holmes. Ed. Martin Harry Greenberg and Carol-Lynn Rössel Waugh (Caroll-Graf hardcover, 1987).

- "Dolan's Cadillac"
  1. *Castle Rock: The Stephen King Newsletter*, February–June 1985.
  2. (Lord John Press edition, 1988).

- "Father's Day"
  Creepshow, 1982.

- "The Fifth Quarter"
  1. *Cavalier*, April 1972. (Written as John Swithen).
  2. *Twilight Zone Magazine*, February 1986. (Reprinted as by Stephen King).

- "For the Birds"
  1. *Bred Any Good Rooks Lately?* Ed. James Charlton (Doubleday trade paperback, 1986).

- "The Glass Floor"
  1. *Startling Mystery Stories*. (Fall 1967).

- "Gramma"
  Skeleton Crew, 1985.

- "Graveyard Shift"
  Night Shift, 1978.

- "Gray Matter"
  Night Shift, 1978.

- "The Gunslinger and the Dark Man"
  The Dark Tower: The Gunslinger (Plume, 1988).

- "The Gunslinger"
  The Dark Tower: The Gunslinger (Plume, 1988).

- "Here There Be Tygers"
  Skeleton Crew, 1985.

- "Home Delivery"
  Book of the Dead, (Bantam paperback, 1989).

- "I Am the Doorway"
  Night Shift, 1978.

- "I Know What You Need"
  Night Shift, 1978.

- "The Jaunt"
  Skeleton Crew, 1985.

- "Jerusalem's Lot"
  Night Shift, 1978.

- "The Last Rung on the Ladder"
  Night Shift, 1978.

- "The Lawnmower Man"
  Night Shift, 1978.

- "The Ledge"
  Night Shift, 1978.

- "The Lonesome Death of Jordy Verrill"
  Creepshow, 1982.

- "The Man Who Loved Flowers"
  Night Shift, 1978.

- "The Man Who Would Not Shake Hands"
  Skeleton Crew, 1985.

- "The Mangler"
  Night Shift, 1978.

- "The Mist"
  Skeleton Crew, 1985.

- "The Monkey"
  Skeleton Crew, 1985.

- "Morning Deliveries (Milkman #1)"
  Skeleton Crew, 1985.

- "Mrs. Todd's Shortcut"
  Skeleton Crew, 1985.

- "My Pretty Pony"
  My Pretty Pony (Alfred A. Knopf hardcover, 1989).

- "The Night Flier"
  Prime Evil. Ed. Douglas E. Winter (New American Library, NAL Books hardcover, 1988; NAL/Signet paperback, 1989).

- "The Night of the Tiger"
  1. *The Magazine of Fantasy and Science Fiction*, February 1978.
  2. *The Year's Best Horror Stories VII* (Daw paperback, 1978).
  3. *The Best Horror Stories from the Magazine of Fantasy and Science Fiction* (Simon and Schuster paperback, 1989).

- "Night Surf"
  Night Shift, 1978.

- "Nona"
  Skeleton Crew, 1985.

- "One for the Road"
  Night Shift, 1978.

- "The Oracle and the Mountains"
  The Dark Tower: The Gunslinger (Plume, 1988).

- "Popsy"
  Masques II. Ed. J. N. Williamson (Maclay hardcover, 1987).
  Best of Masques. Ed. J. N. Williamson (Berkley paperback, 1988).

- "Quitters, Inc."
  Night Shift, 1978.

- "The Raft"
  Skeleton Crew, 1985.

- "Rainy Season"
  Midnight Graffiti, Spring 1989.

- "The Reach"
  Skeleton Crew, 1985.

- "The Reaper's Image"
  Skeleton Crew, 1985.

- "The Reploids"
  Night Visions 5. Ed. Douglas E. Winter (Dark Harvest, 1988).

- "Rita Hayworth and Shawshank Redemption"
  Different Seasons, 1982.

- "The Slow Mutants"
  The Dark Tower: The Gunslinger (Plume, 1988).

- "Sneakers"
  Night Visions 5. Ed. Douglas E. Winter (Dark Harvest, 1988).

- "Something to Tide You Over"
  Creepshow, 1982.

- "Sometimes They Come Back"
  Night Shift, 1978.

- "Strawberry Spring"
  Night Shift, 1978.

- "Suffer the Little Children"
  1. *Cavalier*, February 1972.
  2. *Nightmares.* Ed. Charles L. Grant (Playboy paperback, 1979).

3. *The Evil Image: Two Centuries of Gothic Short Fiction and Poetry*. Eds. Patricia L. Skarda and Nora Crow Jaffe (New American Library, Meridian, 1981).

- "Survivor Type"
  Skeleton Crew, 1985.

- "They're Creeping Up On You"
  Creepshow, 1982.

- "Trucks"
  Night Shift, 1978.

- "Uncle Otto's Truck"
  Skeleton Crew, 1985.

- "The Way Station"
  The Dark Tower: The Gunslinger (Plume, 1988).

- "The Wedding Gig"
  Skeleton Crew, 1985.

- "The Woman in the Room"
  Night Shift, 1978.

- "Word Processor of the Gods"
  Skeleton Crew, 1985.

Other Books of Interest:

- *Danse Macabre* by Stephen King.
  Paperback: New York: Berkley, 1983.
  Incredible. Stephen King, in his only book-length work of nonfiction, takes an unblinking look at horror, and the reader comes away openmouthed with amazement. A very valuable contribution to the genre.

- *Stephen King: The Art of Darkness* by Douglas E. Winter.
  Paperback: New York: New American Library, Signet, 1986.
  A fantastic book that looks at King's life and fiction. Winter is a superb critic—he knows of what he speaks, and his in-depth interpretations of King's novels, themes, subtexts, and style will enlighten and educate you.

• *The Shape Under the Sheet: The Complete Stephen King Encyclopedia* by Stephen J. Spignesi.
Hardcover: Ann Arbor, Mich.: Popular Culture, Ink., 1990.

Just what the title says: An exhaustive encyclopedia covering every person, place and thing in King's fiction. The 17,000 entry annotated concordance will help you with many of the questions in *The Stephen King Quiz Book. The Shape Under the Sheet* also contains mountains of other information, including interviews, photos, and essays on King, his work, and the entire King Phenomenon.

• *The Stephen King Companion* by George Beahm
Trade paperback: Kansas City, Missouri: Andrews and McMeel, 1989.

The *perfect* introductory volume to King and his world. Loaded with articles, interviews, photos and sidebars, the *Companion* gives the novice King reader much-needed information in one compact, nicely-designed volume. The address section and the bibliography are extremely helpful, and after a journey through the *Stephen King Companion*, the reader emerges a more seasoned traveler in the (sometimes daunting) Land of King.

• *Bare Bones*. Ed. by Tim Underwood and Chuck Miller.
Hardcover: New York: McGraw-Hill, 1988.

Huge collection of more than two dozen interviews with King, spanning 1979 through 1985. They're all reprints, but the book is a very valuable resource nonetheless. Many of the interviews included here are now out-of-print and thus, very difficult to find. It's good to have them all in one volume.

• *The Annotated Guide to Stephen King* by Michael R. Collings.
Paperback: Mercer Island, Wash.: Starmont House, 1986.

A *very* comprehensive bibliographic guide to King's work. An invaluable resource.

- *The Shorter Works of Stephen King* by Michael R. Collings and David Engebretson.
  Paperback: Mercer Island, Wash.: Starmont House, 1985.
    An excellent companion to King's shorter work. Good sections on the rare, uncollected materials, too.

- *The Unseen King* by Tyson Blue.
  Paperback: Mercer Island, Wash.: Starmont House, 1985.
    Good introduction to King's rare and uncollected stories.

ALSO . . .
- *Discovering Stephen King*, edited by Darrell Schweitzer.
- *Stephen King as Richard Bachman* by Michael R. Collings.
- *The Many Facets of Stephen King* by Michael R. Collings.
- *The Films of Stephen King* by Michael R. Collings.
- *The Stephen King Phenomenon* by Michael R. Collings.
(All available in paperback from Starmont House.)

- *Stephen King at the Movies* by Jessie Horsting. (NAL/Signet trade paperback, 1986).

Addresses of Sources:

- THE OVERLOOK CONNECTION
P.O. Box 526
Woodstock, Georgia 30188
  Great source for hard-to-find anthologies, first editions, and magazine appearances. They issue a jam-packed catalog loaded with everything from fiction to photos. Dave Hinchberger is the hotel manager and a certified maniac. You'll love Dave and the Overlook.

- TIME TUNNEL
313 Beechwood Avenue
Middlesex, New Jersey 08846
  Craig Goden's *Time Tunnel* is another excellent source for Stephen King-related items. They issue a very comprehensive "newsletter"-type catalog, and their magazine inventory is wide-ranging and complete. *Time Tunnel* stocks some of the harder-to-find items, and I've found them to be very helpful.

• MICHAEL J. AUTREY, BOOKSELLER
13624 Franklin Street, #5
Whittier, California 90602
   Michael specializes in the rarer material, especially
first editions and various unique states of books. His stuff
is somewhat pricey, but he's always got inventory, and
his catalog is very informative and helpful.

• STARMONT HOUSE PUBLISHERS
P.O. Box 851
Mercer Island, Washington 98040
   The publishers of several volumes about King and his
work. Write for a catalog.

• DARK HARVEST PUBLISHERS
P.O. Box 941
Arlington Heights, Illinois 60006
   The publishers of *Night Vision 5* as well as a slew of
other volumes of interest to horror and dark fantasy fans.
Get on their mailing list.

• *Midnight Graffiti*
13101 Sudan Road
Poway, California 92064
   Excellent dark fantasy quarterly. Their third issue was
a Stephen King special, and it contained the first appearance of the King story "Rainy Season." Now with the
demise of *Twilight Zone Magazine*, *Midnight Graffiti* is
one of only a handful of sources left for state-of-the-art
horror and dark fantasy short fiction. The mag is hard to
find on newsstands, so if you don't want to miss out,
SUBSCRIBE! (Jessie'll be glad I said that.)

About the Author

Stephen Spignesi is a New Haven, Connecticut, resident who is addicted to white broccoli pizza and has been known to watch Woody Allen's *Manhattan* in a totally dark room wearing headphones and Ray-Bans.

The *Stephen King Quiz Book* is his second book.

His first book, the "Andy Griffith Show" encyclopedia, *Mayberry, My Hometown* was published in 1987 by Pierian Press.

Stephen's third book is the 1990 release *The Shape Under the Sheet: The Complete Stephen King Encyclopedia*, published by Popular Culture, Ink.

Stephen is married to Pam, who hates horror, (although she *has* read *Carrie* and seen *Beetlejuice*.)

Stephen and Pam have a male long-haired tabby Persian cat named Ben, who was named for Elton John's song "Bennie and the Jets." Stephen didn't realize that Bennie (in the song) was a girl until after the name had been imprinted on his kitty's feline brain pan. To exact revenge, Ben now sheds twelve months of the year.

⊘ SIGNET BOOKS

SPINE TINGLING TALES FROM STEPHEN KING

(0451)

☐ **THE GUNSLINGER.** The first book in *The Dark Tower* series. Roland, the Last Gunslinger, pursues the enigmatic Man in Black across an apocalyptic landscape and toward the forbidding dark tower. This dreamlike tale, the triumph of King's breathtakingly bold imagination, pits the Gunslinger against dark forces. "Compelling."—*Booklist* (160525—$5.95)

☐ **IT.** In Derry, a place as hauntingly familiar as your own hometown, seven teenagers had stumbled upon the horror. Now, grown up, none of them can withstand the force that draws them back to face the nightmare without an end and the evil without a name.... (159276—$5.95)

☐ **PET SEMATARY.** The Creeds were an ideal family, with a charming little daughter and an adorable infant son. When they found the old house in rural Maine, it seemed too good to be true. It was. For the truth was bloodchilling—something more horrifying than death itself, and hideously more powerful . . . (162072—$5.95)

☐ **CUJO.** A big, friendly dog chases a rabbit into a hidden underground cave—and stirs a sleeping evil crueler than death itself. The little Maine town of Castle Rock is about to be invaded by the most hideous menace ever to ravage the flesh and devour the mind . . . (161351—$4.95)

☐ **THE STAND.** The evil started in a laboratory and took over America. Those who died quickly were the lucky ones. Something terrifying was waiting to claim the few scattered survivors—a strange, faceless clairvoyant figure that was reaching for their very souls . . . (160959—$5.95)

☐ **CYCLE OF THE WEREWOLF.** When the moon grows fat, a paralyzing fear sweeps through Tarker Mills. For snarls that sound like human words can be heard whining through the wind. And all around are the footprints of a monster whose hunger cannot be sated . . . (822196—$9.95)

Prices slightly higher in Canada

Buy them at your local bookstore or use this convenient coupon for ordering.

NEW AMERICAN LIBRARY
P.O. Box 999, Bergenfield, New Jersey 07621

Please send me the books I have checked above. I am enclosing $_____ (please add $1.00 to this order to cover postage and handling). Send check or money order—no cash or C.O.D.'s. Prices and numbers are subject to change without notice.

Name_____

Address_____

City _____ State _____ Zip Code _____

Please allow 4-6 weeks for delivery.
This offer is subject to withdrawal without notice.

Ⓢ **SIGNET BOOKS** (0451)

STEPHEN KING TAKES YOU BEYOND TERROR

☐ **SKELETON CREW.** Let Stephen King take you into a world where a macabre mist traps humanity in its swirling horrors... where a beautiful young girl offers satanic seduction... where a child's toy becomes the ultimate instrument of evil... where nothing is what it seems and no escape is possible before the final fearful turn of the page.... (168615—$5.95)

☐ **NIGHT SHIFT.** From the depths of darkness where hideous rats defend their empire, to dizzying heights where a beautiful girl hangs by a hair above a hellish fate, this chilling collection of short stories will plunge you into the subterranean labyrinth of the most spine-tingling, eerie imagination of our time. (160452—$4.95)

☐ **DIFFERENT SEASONS.** An unjustly imprisoned convict, a teenager, four rambunctious young boys, and a disgraced woman are your guides to the ultimate in fascination—to evil, revenge, death, and morality—as Stephen King demonstrates the horror that lurks within. (167538—$5.95)

☐ **CARRIE.** Carrie was not quite aware that she was possessed of a terrifying power. But it was enough to transform a small, quiet New England town into a holocaust of destruction beyond the imagination of man. Innocent schoolgirl or vengeful demon, Carrie will make you shudder.... (157443—$3.95)

☐ **THE EYES OF THE DRAGON by Stephen King. #1 Bestseller.** The ultimate in evil enchantment.... This enthralling masterpiece of magical evil and daring adventure leads you into an irresistible kingdom of wickedness. "Compelling ... his most powerful storytelling!"—*Atlanta Journal constitution* (166582—$4.95)

☐ **'SALEM'S LOT.** The town knew darkness ... and the awful, heavy silence ... and stark white faces ... and the paralyzing fear of a diabolical corruption ... But no one living in 'Salem's Lot dared to talk about the high, sweet, evil laughter of a child ... and the sucking sounds.... (168089—$5.95)

Prices slightly higher in Canada

Buy them at your local bookstore or use this convenient coupon for ordering.

NEW AMERICAN LIBRARY
P.O. Box 999, Bergenfield, New Jersey 07621

Please send me the books I have checked above. I am enclosing $_____
(please add $1.00 to this order to cover postage and handling). Send check or money order—no cash or C.O.D.'s. Prices and numbers are subject to change without notice.

Name_____

Address_____

City _____ State _____ Zip Code _____

Allow 4-6 weeks for delivery.

This offer, prices and numbers are subject to change without notice.